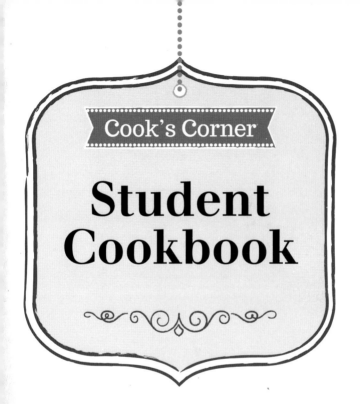

Cook's Corner

Student Cookbook

igloobooks

igloobooks

Published in 2018
by Igloo Books Ltd
Cottage Farm
Sywell
NN6 0BJ
www.igloobooks.com

All imagery: © iStock / Getty Images

STA002 0618
2 4 6 8 10 9 7 5 3
ISBN: 978-1-78810-184-4

Cover designed by Nicholas Gage
Interiors designed by Simon Parker
Edited by Jasmin Peppiatt

Printed and manufactured in China

Cook's Corner

Student Cookbook

Contents

Cook's Corner

Student Cookbook

Breakfasts

Berry and cashew pancakes

SERVES: 4 | PREP TIME: 5 MINUTES | COOKING TIME: 25 MINUTES

INGREDIENTS

250 g / 9 oz / 1⅔ cups plain (all-purpose) flour

2 tsp baking powder

2 large eggs

1 orange, zest finely grated

300 ml / 10 ½ fl. oz / 1 ¼ cups milk

2 tbsp butter

150 g / 5 ½ oz / 1 cup mixed berries

50 g / 1 ¾ oz / ½ cup roasted cashew nuts

icing (confectioner's) sugar for dusting

pouring cream, to serve

METHOD

1. Mix the flour and baking powder in a bowl and make a well in the centre. Break in the eggs, add the orange zest and pour in the milk, then use a whisk to gradually incorporate all of the flour from round the outside.

2. Melt the butter in a small frying pan then whisk it into the batter.

3. Put the buttered frying pan back over a low heat. Spoon the batter into the pan and cook for 2 minutes or until small bubbles start to appear on the surface.

4. Turn the pancakes over with a spatula and cook the other side until golden brown and cooked through.

5. Repeat until all the batter has been used, then stack the pancakes onto plates and garnish with berries and cashews. Sprinkle with icing sugar and serve with a jug of pouring cream on the side.

BLT waffle sandwiches

SERVES: 6 | PREP TIME: 10 MINUTES | COOKING TIME: 25 MINUTES

INGREDIENTS

250 g / 9 oz / 1 ⅔ cups plain (all-purpose) flour

2 tsp baking powder

2 large eggs

300 ml / 10 ½ fl. oz / 1 ¼ cups milk

2 tbsp butter, melted

24 rashers smoked streaky bacon

6 lettuce leaves, halved

4 tomatoes, sliced

METHOD

1. Put the oven on a low setting and put a non-stick electric waffle maker on to heat.

2. Mix the flour and baking powder in a bowl and make a well in the centre. Add the eggs and pour in the milk, then use a whisk to gradually incorporate all of the flour from round the outside. Whisk in the butter.

3. Spoon some of the batter into the waffle maker and close the lid. Cook for 4 minutes or according to the manufacturer's instructions until golden brown. Repeat until all the batter has been used, keeping the finished batches warm in the oven.

4. Meanwhile, fry or grill the bacon until. When the waffles are ready, separate them into quarters and sandwich each pair of quarters together with bacon, lettuce and tomatoes. Serve immediately.

Fresh fruit muesli jars

SERVES: 4 | PREPARATION TIME: 5 MINUTES

INGREDIENTS

125 g / 4 ½ oz / 1 ¼ cups rolled porridge oats

50 g / 1 ¾ oz / ¼ cup whole oat groats

50 g / 1 ¾ oz / ¼ cup flax seeds

50 g / 1 ¾ oz / ¼ cup hulled hemp seeds

50 g / 1 ¾ oz / ¼ cup sunflower seeds

2 tbsp runny honey

500 ml / 17 ½ fl. oz / 2 cups natural yogurt

200 g / 7 oz / 1 ⅓ cups mixed berries, sliced if large

METHOD

1. Toss together the oats, groats, flax, hemp and sunflower seeds in a mixing bowl.

2. Stir the honey into the yogurt, then layer up inside four jars with the oat mix and berries.

Avocado toast with poached egg

SERVES: 1 | PREP TIME: 5 MINUTES | COOKING TIME: 5 MINUTES

INGREDIENTS

1 avocado

1 tsp olive oil

1 egg

3 slices of wholemeal bread.

1 tbsp salted butter

50 g / 1 ¾ oz goats cheese, sliced

Salt and freshly ground black pepper

METHOD

1. Slice the avocado in half and discard the stone. Remove the flesh and slice.

2. Place a pastry ring onto a non-stick frying pan and add the oil. Heat over a moderate heat before breaking the egg into the ring. Cook for 4–5 minutes or until set.

3. Lightly toast the bread, before spreading with the butter.

4. Top the bread with the goats cheese, avocado and egg. Season to taste.

13

Smoked salmon bagels

SERVES: 2 | PREPARATION TIME: 5 MINUTES

INGREDIENTS

2 seeded bagels, halved horizontally

2 tbsp cream cheese

4 slices smoked salmon

1 lemon wedge

2 lettuce leaves

METHOD

1. Spread the bagel bases with cream cheese and arrange the smoked salmon on top.

2. Squeeze a little lemon juice over each one and top with lettuce.

3. Put the bagel tops on top and serve immediately.

Toasted ham and cheese muffin

SERVES: 1 | PREP TIME: 5 MINUTES | COOKING TIME: 5 MINUTES

INGREDIENTS

2 slices Cheddar cheese

1 English breakfast muffin, halved horizontally

3 slices cucumber

3 small slices smoked ham

METHOD

1. Preheat a panini press or toasted sandwich maker.

2. Lay a slice of cheese on the bottom half of the muffin and top with cucumber.

3. Fold the ham slices in half and arrange on top, then add the other slice of cheese and the rest of the muffin.

4. Toast the muffin according to the manufacturer's instructions or until the bread is crisp and the cheese has melted. Serve immediately.

Banana and maple syrup porridge

SERVES: 4 | PREP TIME: 10 MINUTES | COOKING TIME: 8 MINUTES

INGREDIENTS

2 large ripe bananas

600 ml / 1 pint / 2 ½ cups whole milk

125 g / 4 ½ oz / 1 ¼ cups rolled porridge oats

2 tbsp maple syrup, plus extra for drizzling

METHOD

1. Mash one of the bananas and mix with the milk and oats in a saucepan. Stir over a medium heat until it starts to simmer.

2. Add the maple syrup and a pinch of salt then reduce the heat to its lowest setting and continue to stir for 5 minutes.

3. Divide the porridge between four bowls.

4. Slice the other banana and divide between the bowls, then drizzle with extra maple syrup to taste.

Overnight muesli with berries

SERVES: 4 | PREP TIME: 10 MINUTES | COOKING TIME: 8 HOURS

INGREDIENTS

125 g / 4 ½ oz / 1 ¼ cups rolled porridge oats

50 g / 1 ¾ oz / ¼ cup whole oat groats

50 g / 1 ¾ oz / ¼ cup sunflower seeds

50 g / 1 ¾ oz / ¼ cup flax seeds

50 g / 1 ¾ oz / ¼ cup hulled hemp seeds

2 tbsp runny honey

500 ml / 17 ½ fl. oz / 2 cups whole milk,
plus extra to serve

200 g / 7 oz / 1 ⅓ cups mixed berries, sliced if large

100 ml / 3 ½ oz / ½ cup natural yogurt

METHOD

1. Mix the oats with the groats and seeds and
    set aside 2 tablespoons of the dry mix.

2. Stir the honey into the milk to dissolve, then
    stir it into the oat mix. Leave to soak
    overnight in the fridge.

3. Stir the muesli well and divide between four
    bowls, adding a little extra milk to loosen
    if needed.

4. Top each bowl with berries and a spoonful of
    yogurt, then sprinkle with the reserved
    oat mix.

Oat pancakes with strawberries

SERVES: 1-2 | PREP TIME: 15 MINUTES | COOKING TIME: 10 MINUTES

INGREDIENTS

150 g / 5 ¼ oz / 1 ½ cups oats

1 tbsp sugar

1 tsp baking powder

1 egg, beaten

200 ml / 7 fl. oz / ¾ cup milk

1 tbsp oil for frying

100 g / 3 ½ oz fresh strawberries, quartered

50 g / 1 ¾ oz crème fraîche

1 tbsp honey

METHOD

1. Preheat the oven to its lowest setting.

2. Place the oats into a blender and blend to a fine flour.

3. In a large mixing bowl combine the oat flour, sugar and baking powder.

4. Mix the egg and milk and pour into the dry ingredients. Whisk for a couple of minutes until a thick and smooth batter forms. Leave to stand for a couple of minutes.

5. Heat the oil in a non-stick frying pan over a medium high heat. Once hot, add a ladle of the batter to the pan. Allow to form a pancake shape and cook for 2–3 minutes until small holes appear on the surface. Flip over and cook for a further minute before transferring to the oven to keep warm while you cook the remaining batter.

6. Serve the pancakes with the chopped strawberries, a dollop of crème fraîche and a drizzle of honey.

Poached egg and pea toasts

SERVES: 2 | PREP TIME: 5 MINUTES | COOKING TIME: 10 MINUTES

INGREDIENTS

50 g / 1 ¾ oz / ⅓ cup frozen peas or a mixture of peas, broad beans and edamame

2 tbsp white wine vinegar

2 large very fresh eggs

2 slices crusty bread

50 g / 1 ¾ oz / ¼ cup soft goat's cheese

1 handful pea shoots

25 g piece Pecorino or Parmesan

METHOD

1. Bring a wide saucepan of water to the boil and cook the peas and beans for 4 minutes. Transfer to a bowl with a slotted spoon.

2. Reduce the heat of the pan to a gentle simmer and stir in the vinegar.

3. Crack each egg into a cup then pour them smoothly into the water, one at a time. Poach gently for 3 minutes.

4. Toast the bread until golden, then spread with the goat's cheese. Mix the peas and beans with the pea shoots and spoon them on top.

5. Remove the eggs from the pan with a slotted spoon and blot dry with kitchen roll before laying them on the toast.

6. Use a vegetable peeler to shave over the cheese and serve immediately.

20

Strawberry yogurt breakfast pots

SERVES: 1 | PREP TIME: 5 MINUTES | CHILLING TIME: OVERNIGHT

INGREDIENTS

75 g / 2 ½ oz / ½ cup strawberries

1 tsp runny honey

2 tbsp Greek yogurt

½ tsp demerara sugar

METHOD

1. Slice the strawberries and put them in a small preserving jar.

2. Stir the honey into the yogurt and spoon on top, then sprinkle with sugar.

3. Seal the preserving jar and store in the fridge overnight, ready to be enjoyed as a speedy breakfast the next day.

Banana, cranberry and walnut toasties

SERVES: 2 | PREP TIME: 5 MINUTES | COOKING TIME: 2 MINUTES

INGREDIENTS

2 tbsp butter, softened

1 tsp icing (confectioner's) sugar

½ tsp ground cinnamon

2 tbsp walnuts, finely chopped, plus extra to garnish

4 slices white bloomer

2 bananas, halved

50 g / 1 ¾ oz / ¼ cup dried cranberries, plus extra to garnish

mint leaves, to garnish

METHOD

1. Preheat a toasted sandwich maker or put two cast iron frying pans over a medium heat.

2. Mix the butter with the icing sugar, cinnamon and walnuts and spread it over the bread. Sandwich the bread together with the fruit.

3. Toast the sandwiches in the sandwich maker or put them in one of the frying pans and sit the other pan on top. Toast for 2 minutes or until the bread is golden brown.

4. Cut the toasties in half and serve garnished with walnuts, cranberries and mint.

23

Oatmeal with fresh fruit

SERVES: 1 | PREP TIME: 5 MINUTES | COOKING TIME: 15 MINUTES

INGREDIENTS

400 ml / 13 ½ fl. oz / 1 ⅔ cups almond milk

50 g / 1 ¾ oz / ½ cup oatmeal

1 tbsp organic honey

½ banana, sliced

2 strawberries, sliced

1 tbsp hazlenuts, chopped

METHOD

1. Place the milk into a saucepan and heat until boiling.

2. Gradually add the oatmeal stirring continuously.

3. Once all the oatmeal has been added turn down to a simmer for 12–15 minutes until hot and at your preferred thickness.

4. Stir through the honey before placing into a serving bowl and topping with the remaining ingredients.

Strawberry and banana waffles

SERVES: 2 | PREPARATION TIME: 20 MINUTES

INGREDIENTS

100 g / 3 ½ oz strawberries

568 ml / 19 ¼ fl. oz / 2 ¼ cups double (heavy) cream

8 stroopwafels

1 banana, sliced

1 tbsp strawberry jam (jelly)

METHOD

1. Dehull the strawberries and slice into thirds or quarters depending on the size of the berry.

2. Whip the cream until thickened. Spoon into a piping bag with a star nozzle.

3. Create the dessert by topping a waffle with strawberries and cream, place a second waffle on top with banana and cream and then another strawberry layer.

4. Top the dessert with some cream, a strawberry and a drop of strawberry jam.

Baked avocado eggs

SERVES: 2 | PREP TIME: 10 MINUTES | COOKING TIME: 20 MINUTES

INGREDIENTS

2 avocados, halved and stoned

4 medium eggs

1 tbsp parsley, finely chopped

METHOD

1. Preheat the oven to 220°C (200°C fan) / 425F / gas 7.

2. Enlarge the stone cavity of the avocados with a teaspoon to make space for the eggs.

3. Arrange the avocados cut side up in a snug baking dish and break an egg into the middle of each one.

4. Season with salt and pepper, then bake for 18 minutes or until the egg whites have set, but the yolks are still a little runny.

5. Sprinkle with parsley and serve immediately.

Homemade granola with fresh berries

MAKES: 6-8 | PREP TIME: 5 MINUTES | COOKING TIME: 20 MINUTES

INGREDIENTS

150 g / 5 ¼ oz / ½ cup pure maple syrup

2 tbsp raw honey

2 tbsp coconut oil

1 tsp vanilla extract

300 g / 10 ½ oz / 3 cups whole rolled oats

100 g / 3 ½ oz / ¾ cup pumpkin seeds

100 g / 3 ½ oz / ¾ cup sunflower seeds

100 g / 3 ½ oz/ ¾ cup pecan pieces

Fresh berries and yogurt to serve

METHOD

1. Preheat the oven to 150°C (130°C fan) / 300F / gas 2. Mix together the syrup, honey, oil and vanilla extract in a large bowl. Pour in the oats, seeds and nuts and mix to combine.

2. Tip the granola mixture onto a baking tray and spread evenly, use two if required, and place in the oven to bake for 20 minutes, turning the mixture over once during cooking.

3. Remove from the oven and leave to cool.

4. Serve the granola with natural yogurt and fresh berries as desired.

27

Cheese and herb omelette

SERVES: 1 | PREP TIME: 5 MINUTES | COOKING TIME: 10 MINUTES

INGREDIENTS

1 tsp butter

4 eggs, whisked

50 g / 1 ¾ oz / ½ cup grated cheese

1 tsp dried oregano

METHOD

1. Preheat the grill to a medium setting.

2. In a non-stick frying pan heat the butter over a medium high heat.

3. Once bubbling, add the whisked eggs and swill around the pan so that they cover the entire base. Season with salt and black pepper.

4. Cook for 4–5 minutes until crisp on the bottom. Add the cheese and oregano over the surface.

5. Transfer the pan to the grill and grill until the cheese has melted.

6. Remove from the grill and place onto a serving plate.

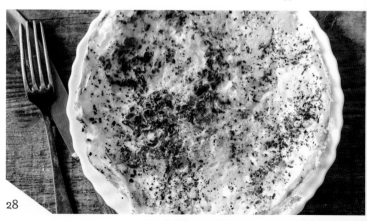

Scrambled egg on toast

SERVES: 2 | PREP TIME: 5 MINUTES | COOKING TIME: 5 MINUTES

INGREDIENTS

2 slices granary bread

2 tbsp butter, softened

4 large eggs

METHOD

1. Toast the bread in a toaster or under a hot grill until golden brown. Spread with half the butter and keep warm.

2. Gently beat the eggs with a pinch of salt and pepper to break up the yolks.

3. Heat the rest of the butter in a non-stick frying pan until sizzling then pour in the eggs.

4. Cook over a low heat, stirring constantly until the eggs start to scramble. As soon as it reaches your favourite scramble consistency, divide it between the two slices of toast and serve immediately.

Banana and walnut pancakes

SERVES: 4 | PREP TIME: 15 MINUTES | COOKING TIME: 30 MINUTES

INGREDIENTS

250 g / 9 oz / 1 ⅔ cups plain (all purpose) flour

2 tsp baking powder

4 very ripe bananas

2 large eggs

225 ml / 8 fl. oz / ¾ cups milk

2 tbsp melted butter

50 g / 1 ¾ oz / ½ cup walnuts, chopped

125 ml / 4 ½ fl. oz / ½ cup golden syrup

METHOD

1. Mix the flour and baking powder in a bowl and make a well in the centre.

2. Mash two of the bananas with a fork until smooth, then whisk in the eggs and milk. Gradually whisk the mixture into the flour bowl. Melt the butter in a frying pan then whisk it into the batter. Put the buttered frying pan back over a low heat.

3. Spoon heaped tablespoons of the batter into the pan and cook for 2 minutes or until small bubbles start to appear on the surface. Turn the pancakes over with a spatula and cook the other side until golden brown and cooked through.

4. Repeat until all the batter has been used, keeping the finished batches warm in a low oven.

5. Stack the pancakes on warm plates. Slice the other two bananas and arrange on top with the walnuts, then drizzle with golden syrup.

Cook's Corner

Student Cookbook

Main meals

Beef enchiladas

SERVES: 4 | PREP TIME: 20 MINUTES | COOKING TIME: 50 MINUTES

INGREDIENTS

200 g / 7 oz / 1 cup long grain rice

1 tbsp olive oil

1 onion, diced

250 g / 9 oz beef mince

1 tsp chilli (chili) powder

1 tsp smoked paprika

1 tsp ground cumin

1 tsp ground coriander (cilantro)

4 tortilla wraps

500 g / 1 lb 1 oz passata

2 red chillies (chili), sliced

150 g / 5 ¼ oz / ½ cup mozzarella cheese, grated

150 g / 5 ¼ oz / ½ cup cheddar cheese, grated

METHOD

1. Preheat the oven to 180°C (160°C fan) / 350F / gas 4.

2. Cook the rice as per the packet instructions, set aside until needed.

3. Heat the oil over a medium high heat in a large casserole dish. Add the onion and cook for 5-10 minutes until softened. Add the beef mince and brown before adding the chilli powder, paprika, cumin and coriander. Fry for a further minute until fragrant before adding a splash of water. Cover and cook for 8–10 minutes before mixing through the rice.

4. Spoon the rice and beef mixture into the tortillas before rolling to seal and placing into an oven proof dish.

5. Pour over the passata and scatter over the chillies and grated cheeses.

6. Bake in the oven for 30 minutes until the cheese has melted and the tortillas are crisp.

Chicken dippers and chips

SERVES: 4 | PREP TIME: 1 HOUR 45 MINUTES | COOKING TIME: 20 MINUTES

INGREDIENTS

4 large Maris Piper potatoes, peeled and cut into skinny chips

200 g / 7 oz / 1 ⅓ cups plain (all-purpose)

2 tbsp olive oil

250 ml / 9 fl. oz / 1 cup pale ale

4 skinless chicken breasts, sliced lengthways

sunflower oil for deep-frying

mayonnaise, to serve

METHOD

1. Soak the potatoes in cold water for 1 hour to reduce the starch.

2. Drain the chips and dry completely with a clean tea towel, then air-dry on a wire rack for 30 minutes.

3. Meanwhile, make the batter. Sieve the flour into a bowl then whisk in the oil and ale until smoothly combined.

4. Heat the oil in a deep fat fryer, according to the manufacturer's instructions, to a temperature of 130°C (265F). Par-cook the chips for 10 minutes so that they cook all the way through but don't brown. Drain the chips on plenty of kitchen paper to absorb the excess oil.

5. Increase the fryer temperature to 180°C (350F). Dip the chicken in the batter and fry for 6 minutes or until golden brown. Transfer the chicken to a kitchen paper lined bowl and increase the fryer temperature to 190°C (375F).

6. Return the chips to the fryer basket and cook for 4 minutes or until crisp and golden brown. Drain the chips of excess oil and serve straight away with the chicken and some mayonnaise for dipping.

Creamy mushroom tagliatelle

SERVES: 2 | PREP TIME: 5 MINUTES | COOKING TIME: 15 MINUTES

INGREDIENTS

2 tbsp olive oil

1 tbsp butter

200 g / 7 oz / 2 ⅔ cups mushrooms, sliced

1 tbsp rosemary

1 tbsp thyme

2 cloves of garlic, finely chopped

200 ml / 7 fl. oz / ¾ cup double cream

200 g / 7 oz / 2 cups tagliatelle

50 g / 1 ¾ oz / ½ cup Parmesan, finely grated

METHOD

1. Heat the oil and butter in a sauté pan and fry the mushrooms and herbs until any liquid evaporates and the mushrooms start to colour.

2. Add the garlic and cook for 2 more minutes, stirring all the time, then add the cream and bring to a gentle simmer.

3. While the sauce is cooking, boil the tagliatelle in salted water until al dente. Drain well.

4. Stir the Parmesan into the sauce, then toss with the tagliatelle and serve on two warm plates.

Beef with spring onion

SERVES: 4 | PREP TIME: 5 MINUTES | COOKING TIME: 10 MINUTES

INGREDIENTS

1 small head broccoli, broken into florets

2 tbsp sunflower oil

1 clove of garlic, chopped

1 tbsp fresh root ginger, chopped

4 spring onions (scallions), chopped, with green and white parts separated

1 large sirloin steak, thinly sliced

60 ml / 2 fl. oz / ¼ cup oyster sauce

steamed rice to serve

METHOD

1. Boil or steam the broccoli for 3 minutes or until tender, then drain and set aside.

2. Heat the oil in a large wok and fry the garlic, ginger and spring onion whites for 1 minute.

3. Add the steak and stir-fry for 3 minutes or until it starts to colour.

4. Pour in the oyster sauce, adding a splash of water if the sauce is too thick. Stir-fry for 1 minute, then toss with the broccoli and spring onion greens.

5. Serve immediately on a bed of steamed rice.

39

Fishcakes with dill

SERVES: 6 | PREP TIME: 10 MINUTES | CHILLING TIME: 1 HOUR
COOKING TIME: 6 MINUTES

INGREDIENTS

225 g / 8 oz / 1 ½ cups skinless, boneless pollock fillet, cubed

225 g / 8 oz / 1 ½ cups skinless boneless salmon fillet, cubed

100 g / 3 ½ oz / 1 ⅓ cups fresh white breadcrumbs

1 large egg, plus 1 egg yolk

1 small bunch dill, chopped

1 tsp Dijon mustard

2 tbsp plain (all-purpose) flour

2 tbsp sunflower oil

METHOD

1. Put all of the ingredients, except for the flour, in a food processor with a pinch of salt and black pepper. Pulse until finely chopped and evenly mixed.

2. Flour your hands and shape the mixture into six patties. Chill in the fridge for at least 1 hour.

3. Heat the oil in a frying pan. Depending on the size of the pan, you may need to cook the fishcakes in batches. Fry the fishcakes over a medium-low heat for 3 minutes on each side or until cooked through. Serve immediately.

Easy focaccia pizza

MAKES: 1 | PREP TIME: 5 MINUTES | COOKING TIME: 10 MINUTES

INGREDIENTS

1 oval focaccia

2 tbsp tomato pizza sauce

150 g / 5 ½ oz / 1 cup mini mozzarella balls, halved

8 cherry tomatoes, halved

½ tsp dried oregano

1 handful basil leaves

METHOD

1. Preheat the oven to 200°C (180°C fan) / 400F / gas 6.

2. Lay the focaccia on a baking tray and spread with tomato pizza sauce.

3. Top with mozzarella and tomatoes, then scatter with oregano and basil leaves.

4. Bake the pizza for 10 minutes or until the cheese has melted and the tomatoes are soft.

5. Cut into slices and serve immediately.

Tomato soup

SERVES: 4 | PREP TIME: 5 MINUTES | COOKING TIME: 30 MINUTES

INGREDIENTS

2 tbsp olive oil

1 onion, finely chopped

3 cloves of garlic, crushed

400 g / 14 oz / 2 cups canned tomatoes, chopped

500 ml / 17 ½ fl. oz / 2 cups vegetable stock

1 tsp caster (superfine) sugar

Greek yogurt and fresh chives, to serve

METHOD

1. Heat the oil in a saucepan and fry the onion for 8 minutes or until softened.

2. Add the garlic and cook for 2 more minutes, then stir in the tomatoes and vegetable stock and bring to the boil.

3. Simmer for 20 minutes, then blend until smooth with a liquidizer or immersion blender.

4. Taste the soup and adjust the seasoning with sugar, salt and pepper.

5. Ladle into bowls and garnish with yogurt, chives and black pepper.

Fusilli pasta salad

SERVES: 4 | PREP TIME: 5 MINUTES | COOKING TIME: 12 MINUTES

INGREDIENTS

400 g / 14 oz / 4 cups fusilli pasta

50 ml / 1 ¾ fl. oz / ¼ cup olive oil

1 lemon, juiced

150 g / 5 ½ oz / ⅔ cup sundried tomatoes in oil

100 g / 3 ½ oz / ½ cup capers in brine, drained

2 large handfuls mixed salad leaves

2 tbsp pine nuts, toasted

30 g Parmesan

METHOD

1. Boil the pasta in salted water according to the packet instructions or until al dente.

2. Drain the pasta, then plunge into iced water to cool. Drain well.

3. Toss the pasta with the rest of the ingredients, except for the Parmesan and season to taste with salt and pepper.

4. Use a vegetable peeler to shave over the Parmesan just before serving.

Ham, cheese and salad sandwiches

SERVES: 2 | PREP TIME: 5 MINUTES | COOKING TIME: 2 MINUTES

INGREDIENTS

4 thick slices white bloomer

2 tbsp mayonnaise

2 lettuce leaves

1 tomato, sliced

4 slices smoked ham

6 slices cucumber

4 slices Emmental cheese

1 handful pea shoots

METHOD

1. Heat a griddle pan until smoking hot, then toast the bread on one side until attractively marked.

2. Spread the untoasted side with mayonnaise and top two of the slices with lettuce, tomato, ham, cucumber, Emmental and pea shoots.

3. Put the other slices of bread on top, then cut in half and secure with cocktail sticks.

44

Spicy chicken bites

SERVES: 2 | PREP TIME: 15 MINUTES | COOKING TIME: 15 MINUTES

INGREDIENTS

300 g / 10 ½ oz chicken breast, diced

2 tbsp soy sauce

1 tsp rice wine vinegar

1 tsp chilli (chili) flakes

1 clove of garlic, minced

1 tsp cornflour (cornstarch)

1 lemon, juiced

1 tsp sesame oil

METHOD

1. Preheat the oven to 200°C (180°C fan) / 400F / gas 6.

2. Place the chicken into a mixing bowl.

3. Whisk together the remaining ingredients and pour over the chicken. Toss the chicken to coat in the sauce. Leave for 10 minutes to marinade.

4. Pour the chicken and sauce onto a baking tray and place into the oven for 15 minutes.

5. Spoon the chicken into serving bowls with some steamed rice or vegetables.

45

Penne with slow cooked pork

SERVES: 4-6 | PREP TIME: 15 MINUTES | COOKING TIME: 4 HOURS

INGREDIENTS

800 g / 1 lb 12 oz pork shoulder joint, boneless

1 tbsp dried oregano

1 tbsp olive oil

1 onion, diced

150 g / 5 ¼ oz chestnut mushrooms, chopped

2 cloves of garlic, chopped

500 ml / 17 fl. oz / 2 cups beef stock

200 ml / 7 fl. oz / ¾ cup red wine

500 g / 1 lb 1 oz penne pasta

handful of chives, chopped

METHOD

1. Preheat the oven to 160°C (140°C fan) / 325F / gas 3.

2. Rub the pork all over with the oregano and season with salt and black pepper.

3. Heat the oil in a casserole dish large enough to hold the meat. Add the onion and fry for 4–5 minutes until softened. Add the mushrooms and garlic, frying for a further 3–4 minutes until the mushrooms have started to colour a little.

4. Add the pork to the pan and brown all over. Pour over the stock and wine before increasing the heat until boiling. Cover and then place into the oven for up to 4 hours, seasoning with salt and black pepper to taste.

5. Remove the pork from the oven and place the meat into a roasting tray. Pull the meat apart using forks until shredded. Return to the casserole dish and stir through the sauce. If the sauce is watery, dissolve some cornflour in water and mix through to thicken. Place onto the hob to keep warm.

6. Cook the pasta as per the packet instructions, drain and return to the pan.

7. Mix the pork through the pasta before placing into serving bowls and garnishing with the chopped chives.

Pumpkin cream soup

SERVES: 1-2 | PREP TIME: 15 MINUTES | COOKING TIME: 30 MINUTES

INGREDIENTS

1 medium sized pumpkin

1 tbsp olive oil

1 onion, diced

2 cloves of garlic, minced

200 ml / 7 fl. oz / ¾ cup vegetable stock

100 ml / 3 ½ fl. oz / ½ cup double (heavy) cream

handful of fresh basil, chopped

croutons to serve

METHOD

1. Preheat the oven to 180°C (160°C fan) / 350F / gas 4.

2. Cut the top off the pumpkin and scoop out the flesh and seeds. Separate the seeds from the flesh.

3. Place the flesh onto a baking tray and place into the oven and roast for 20 minutes until tender.

4. Meanwhile, heat the oil in a saucepan over a medium heat. Add the onion and fry for 4–6 minutes until softened. Add the garlic and fry for a further minute until fragrant.

5. Add the roast pumpkin to the pan and pour in the stock. Blend with a hand blender until smooth. Pour in three quarters of the cream and season with salt and pepper before blending again to mix through.

6. Heat a dry frying pan over a medium heat and toast the pumpkin seeds for 4–5 minutes until you can smell them. Remove from the heat and set aside.

7. Spoon the cooked soup back into the pumpkin and add a swirl of cream. Top with the toasted pumpkin seeds, croutons and chopped basil.

Baked eggs with tomato

SERVES: 2 | PREP TIME: 10 MINUTES | COOKING TIME: 10 MINUTES

INGREDIENTS

100 g / 3 ½ oz cherry tomatoes, halved

1 shallot, diced

1 clove of garlic, minced

2 tbsp olive oil

2 large free-range eggs

handful of chopped basil

METHOD

1. Preheat the oven to 180°C (160°C fan) / 350F / gas 4.

2. Combine the tomatoes, shallot, garlic and oil in a bowl. Season with salt and black pepper and toss to combine.

3. Spoon the tomato mixture into ramekins before carefully breaking an egg over the top.

4. Bake in the hot oven for 8–10 minutes or until the egg white has set.

5. Remove and scatter over the fresh basil and a little more cracked black pepper.

Salmon and vegetable bake

SERVES: 2 | PREP TIME: 10 MINUTES | COOKING TIME: 25 MINUTES

INGREDIENTS

2 thick salmon steaks

175 g / 6 oz / 1 ½ cups broccoli, broken into small florets

200 g / 7 oz / 1 ⅔ cups baby sprouts

6 cherry tomatoes

3 small shallots, cut into wedges

½ lemon

2 sprigs rosemary

50 ml / 1 ¾ fl. oz / ¼ cup olive oil

1 tbsp fresh thyme, chopped

½ tsp mixed peppercorns, crushed

METHOD

1. Preheat the oven to 200°C (180°C fan) / 400F / gas 6.

2. Arrange the salmon steaks in a baking dish and surround with the broccoli, sprouts, tomatoes and shallots.

3. Cut a slice from the lemon, then cut it in half and use to garnish the salmon with the rosemary. Squeeze the rest of the lemon half, then whisk in the oil, thyme, peppercorns and a little salt.

4. Drizzle the mixture all over the salmon and vegetables, then bake for 25 minutes or until the fish is just cooked in the centre and the vegetables are tender.

Tortilla rolls

SERVES: 1 | PREPARATION TIME: 10 MINUTES

INGREDIENTS

1 tortilla

1 avocado, peeled and destoned

¼ cucumber, cut into ribbons

1 tomato, sliced

1 slice of flexible or rubbery cheese,
such as Emmental or Jarlsberg

METHOD

1. Place the tortilla onto a clean and dry surface.

2. Finely slice the avocado and place onto the tortilla.

3. Top with the ribbons of cucumber and sliced tomato.

4. Place the cheese in the centre of the tortilla.

5. Fold the tortilla over the contents and roll into a tube.

6. Slice in half and serve.

Triple-decker sandwich

SERVES: 1 | PREPARATION TIME: 5 MINUTES

INGREDIENTS

4 slices wholemeal bread

1 tbsp soft goat's cheese

2 lettuce leaves

1 tsp mustard

4 slices wafer thin smoked ham

1 tbsp mayonnaise

6 slices cucumber

4 slices tomato

METHOD

1. Spread one slice of the bread with goat's cheese and top with one of the lettuce leaves.

2. Add a second slice of bread and spread with mustard. Top with the ham.

3. Add a third slice of bread and spread with half of the mayonnaise. Top with cucumber and tomato, followed by the other lettuce leaf.

4. Spread the underside of the final slice of bread with the rest of the mayonnaise and lay it on top, then hold everything together with a wooden skewer.

Vegetarian chilli

SERVES: 6 | PREP TIME: 5 MINUTES | COOKING TIME: 40 MINUTES

INGREDIENTS

2 tbsp olive oil

1 onion, finely chopped

2 cloves of garlic, crushed

½ tsp cayenne pepper

450 g / 1 lb / 3 cups veggie mince

400 g / 14 oz / 2 cups canned tomatoes, chopped

200 ml / 7 fl. oz / ¾ cup vegetable stock

400 g / 14 oz / 2 cups canned mixed beans, drained

200 g / 7 oz / 1 cup canned sweetcorn, drained

100 g / 3 ½ oz / 1 cup Double Gloucester cheese, grated

100 g / 3 ½ oz / 1 cup Cheddar, grated

2 tbsp coriander (cilantro), chopped

lime wedges and tortilla chips to serve

METHOD

1. Heat the oil in a large saucepan and fry the onion for 5 minutes, stirring occasionally. Add the garlic and cayenne and cook for 2 minutes, then add the mince.

2. Fry the mince until it starts to brown, then add the chopped tomatoes, stock, beans and sweetcorn and bring to a gentle simmer.

3. Cook for 30 minutes, stirring occasionally, until the mince is tender and the sauce has thickened a little. Season to taste with salt and pepper.

4. Divide the chilli between six warm bowls. Mix the two cheeses together and sprinkle on top with the coriander, then serve with lime wedges and tortilla chips on the side.

Chicken fajita bake

SERVES: 4 | PREP TIME: 20 MINUTES | COOKING TIME: 40 MINUTES

INGREDIENTS

2 tbsp olive oil

1 onion, finely chopped

2 cloves of garlic, crushed

2 red chillies (chilies), finely chopped

400 g / 14 oz / 2 cups fresh or canned tomatoes, chopped

300 g / 10 ½ oz / 2 cups leftover cooked chicken, sliced

8 flour tortillas

100 g / 3 ½ oz / 1 cup Cheddar cheese, grated

1 handful parsley, chopped

METHOD

1. Preheat the oven to 220°C (200°C fan) / 425F / gas 7.

2. Heat the oil in a saucepan and fry the onion for 5 minutes, stirring occasionally. Add the garlic and chillies, then cook for an additional 2 minutes.

3. Add the tomatoes and a splash of water and simmer for 15 minutes.

4. Tip half of the tomato sauce into a bowl and set aside. Add the chicken to the saucepan and warm through.

5. Divide the chicken mixture between the tortillas and roll them up tightly. Arrange in a snug single layer in a baking dish. Pour the reserved tomato sauce over the top and scatter with cheese and parsley.

6. Bake in the oven for 15 minutes or until the cheese is fully melted and bubbling.

Forager's vegetable stew

SERVES: 4 | PREP TIME: 5 MINUTES | COOKING TIME: 5 MINUTES

INGREDIENTS

2 tbsp olive oil

1 onion, finely chopped

1 celery stick, finely chopped

1 carrot, cubed

150 g / 5 ½ oz / ¾ cup pearl barley

1 litre / 1 pint 15 fl. oz / 4 cups vegetable stock

2 large potatoes, peeled and cubed

30 g / 1 oz / 1 cup stinging nettles, picked with gloves and chopped

30 g / 1 oz / 1 cup ransom (wild garlic), chopped

wholemeal bread, to serve

METHOD

1. Heat the oil in a large saucepan and gently fry the onion, celery and carrot for 5 minutes without colouring.

2. Stir in the barley then pour in the stock and bring to the boil.

3. Turn the heat down and simmer the stew for 25 minutes.

4. Add the potatoes and continue to simmer for 20 minutes or until the barley and potatoes are tender.

5. Add the nettles and ransom to the pan and simmer for 1 minute or until they just start to wilt, then season to taste with salt and pepper.

6. Ladle the stew into four bowls and serve with wholemeal bread.

Blue cheese risotto

SERVES: 2 | PREP TIME: 10 MINUTES | COOKING TIME: 35 MINUTES

INGREDIENTS

1 litre / 1 pint 15 fl. oz / 4 cups vegetable stock

2 tbsp olive oil

1 onion, finely chopped

2 cloves of garlic, crushed

150 g / 5 ½ oz / ¾ cup risotto rice

2 tbsp butter

150 g / 5 ½ oz / 1 cup blue cheese, diced

1 handful basil leaves

METHOD

1. Heat the stock in a saucepan and keep it just below simmering point.

2. Heat the olive oil in a sauté pan and gently fry the onion for 5 minutes without colouring. Add the garlic and cook for 2 more minutes then stir in the rice.

3. When it is well coated with the oil, add two ladles of the hot stock.

4. Cook, stirring occasionally, until most of the stock has been absorbed before adding the next two ladles. Continue in this way for around 20 minutes or until the rice is just tender.

5. Stir in the butter, then cover the pan and take off the heat to rest for 4 minutes.

6. Fold through the blue cheese and half of the basil, then season to taste with salt and pepper. Divide between two warm bowls, scatter over the rest of the basil and serve immediately.

Homemade burgers

SERVES: 4 | PREP TIME: 20 MINUTES | COOKING TIME: 8 MINUTES

INGREDIENTS

450 g / 1 lb / 2 cups minced beef, not too lean

2 tbsp double cream

1 tsp Dijon mustard

2 tbsp sunflower oil

4 seeded burger buns, halved horizontally

2 tbsp mayonnaise

½ red onion, sliced

4 gherkins, sliced

50 g / 1 ¾ oz / 1 ½ cups mixed salad leaves

1 large tomato, sliced

METHOD

1. Mix the mince with the cream and mustard and season generously with salt and pepper, then knead lightly until sticky. Divide the mixture into four and compress each one into a tight patty with your hands.

2. Heat the oil in a frying pan then fry the burgers for 8 minutes, turning every 2 minutes.

3. Spread the bun bases with mayonnaise and top with sliced onion.

4. Sit the burgers on top when they're ready and garnish with gherkin, salad leaves and tomato before adding the tops of the buns.

Prawn tacos

SERVES: 2 | PREP TIME: 10 MINUTES | COOKING TIME: 25 MINUTES

INGREDIENTS

4 mini tortillas

120 g / 4 ¼ oz king prawns, shelled removes

1 tsp paprika

1 tsp cayenne

1 lemon, juiced

1 tbsp olive oil

1 red chilli (chili), finely chopped

1 clove of garlic, minced

handful of fresh coriander (cilantro), chopped

150 g / 5 ¼ oz coleslaw

METHOD

1. Preheat the oven to 180°C (160°C fan) / 350F / gas 4.

2. Turn a muffin tin upside down and place the tortillas into the gaps so that they form a taco shape. Bake in the oven for 18-20 minutes until crisp and holding their shape.

3. Combine the prawns with the paprika, cayenne and lemon juice.

4. Heat the oil in a frying pan over a medium high heat. Add the chilli and garlic and fry for 2–3 minutes until fragrant. Add the prawns and continue to cook until pink, then add the coriander to the pan and toss to coat the prawns.

5. Serve the prawns in the taco shells with the coleslaw and your favourite sauces.

63

Chicken wings with roast new potatoes

SERVES: 4 | PREP TIME: 15 MINUTES | COOKING TIME: 45 MINUTES

INGREDIENTS

1 tbsp honey
1 lemon, juiced
2 cloves of garlic, minced
1 tsp paprika
1 tbsp tomato puree
2 tbsp olive oil
800 g / 1 lb 12 oz chicken wings
500 g / 1 lb 1 oz new potatoes
handful of basil leaves

METHOD

1. Preheat the oven to 200°C (180°C fan) / 400F / gas 6.

2. Whisk together the honey, lemon, garlic, paprika, tomato and olive oil in a large mixing bowl. Add the chicken wings and toss to coat in the marinade.

3. Place the chicken wings into a roasting tray along with the potatoes. Season with salt and black pepper before roasting in the oven for 40–45 minutes.

4. Remove from the oven and scatter the basil leaves before serving.

64

Lentil stew

SERVES: 4 | PREP TIME: 5 MINUTES | COOKING TIME: 50 MINUTES

INGREDIENTS

50 ml / 1 ¾ fl. oz / ¼ cup olive oil

2 leeks, sliced

4 small carrots, cut into chunks

2 cloves of garlic, sliced

1 tbsp tomato puree

1 litre / 1 pint 15 fl. oz / 4 cups vegetable stock

400 g / 14 oz / 3 ¼ cups green lentils

2 bay leaves

mint sprigs, to garnish

METHOD

1. Heat the oil in a large saucepan and fry the leeks, carrots and garlic for 5 minutes.

2. Stir in the tomato puree, stock, lentils and bay leaves, then simmer for 45 minutes or until the lentils are tender. If the liquid evaporates too quickly, add a little boiling water.

3. Taste for seasoning and add salt and black pepper as necessary then discard the bay leaves.

4. Divide between four warm bowls and serve garnished with mint.

Spinach soup

SERVES: 4 | PREP TIME: 10 MINUTES | COOKING TIME: 30 MINUTES

INGREDIENTS

1 tbsp olive oil

2 tbsp butter

2 leeks, chopped

2 cloves of garlic, crushed

2 potatoes, peeled and diced

1 litre / 1 pint 15 fl. oz / 4 cups vegetable stock

¼ tsp nutmeg, freshly grated

200 g / 7 oz / 6 cups spinach, washed

Greek yogurt, to serve

METHOD

1. Heat the oil and butter in a saucepan and fry the leeks for 8 minutes or until softened.

2. Add the garlic and potatoes to the pan and cook for 2 more minutes, then stir in the vegetable stock and bring to the boil.

3. Simmer for 15 minutes or until the potatoes are tender, then adjust the seasoning with nutmeg, salt and black pepper.

4. Stir the spinach into the pan, a couple of handfuls at a time, waiting for it to wilt down before adding the next batch.

5. As soon as it has all been incorporated, transfer the soup to a liquidizer and blend until very smooth.

6. Serve the soup in bowls with a dollop of yogurt on the top.

Potato and spinach tortilla

SERVES: 4 | PREP TIME: 10 MINUTES | COOKING TIME: 20 MINUTES

INGREDIENTS

75 ml / 2 ½ oz / ⅓ cup olive oil

1 onion, thinly sliced

50 g / 1 ¾ oz / 1 ½ cups baby leaf spinach, washed

4 small boiled potatoes, cooled and sliced

6 large eggs

METHOD

1. Heat half the oil in a non-stick frying pan and fry the onion with a pinch of salt and pepper for 5 minutes. Add the spinach to the pan and cook until it has wilted and any liquid has evaporated.

2. Meanwhile, gently beat the eggs in a jug to break up the yolks.

3. When the spinach is ready, stir it into the eggs with the potatoes and season with salt and pepper.

4. Heat the rest of the oil in the frying pan then pour in the egg mixture.

5. Cook over a gentle heat for 6–8 minutes or until the egg has set round the outside, but the centre is still a bit soft.

6. Turn it out onto a plate, then slide it back into the pan and cook the other side for 4–6 minutes.

7. Leave to cool for 5 minutes before serving.

Penne with mushrooms

SERVES: 4 | PREP TIME: 5 MINUTES | COOKING TIME: 12 MINUTES

INGREDIENTS

400 g / 14 oz / 4 cups penne pasta

75 ml / 2 ½ fl. oz / ⅓ cup olive oil

300 g / 10 ½ oz / 3 cups shimeji or baby chestnut mushrooms

2 cloves of garlic, crushed

100 ml / 3 ½ fl. oz / ½ cup dry white wine

100 g / 3 ½ oz / 1 cup Pecorino Romano or Parmesan, grated

2 handfuls rocket (arugula)

METHOD

1. Boil the pasta in salted water according to the packet instructions or until al dente.

2. Meanwhile, heat the oil in a large sauté pan and fry the mushrooms for 8 minutes.

3. Add the garlic and stir-fry for 1 minute, then pour in the wine and bubble until reduced by half.

4. Drain the pasta and toss with the mushrooms. Divide between four warm bowls and scatter over the cheese and rocket.

Chunky tomato soup

SERVES: 2-4 | PREP TIME: 15 MINUTES | COOKING TIME: 30 MINUTES

INGREDIENTS

2 tbsp olive oil, plus more to drizzle

1 onion, sliced

2 cloves of garlic, minced

150 g / 5 ¼ oz cherry tomatoes, quartered

400 g / 14 oz canned peeled plum tomatoes

handful of fresh basil, chopped

METHOD

1. Heat the oil in a heavy based saucepan. Add the onions and cook for 5–6 minutes until softened. Add the garlic to the pan and cook for a further minute until fragrant.

2. Add the cherry tomatoes and mix through the onions and garlic. Cook for 2–3 minutes before adding the plum tomatoes and juice. Top up with water by half filling the plum tomato can and pouring into the saucepan.

3. Heat until boiling and then turn down to a simmer, add most of the basil and leave to cook for 20 minutes.

4. Season to taste and cook for longer if needed. Spoon into serving bowls and drizzle over some more oil.

Chicken escalopes with vegetable rice

SERVES: 1 | PREP TIME: 15 MINUTES | COOKING TIME: 30 MINUTES

INGREDIENTS

75 g / 2 ½ oz / ⅓ cup long grain rice

1 chicken breast

50 g / 1 ¾ oz / ⅓ cup panko breadcrumbs, lightly crushed

50 g / 1 ¾ oz / ½ cup parmesan, grated

1 tbsp flour, seasoned

1 egg beaten

2 tbsp olive oil

75 g / 2 ½ oz mixed frozen vegetables

METHOD

1. Cook the rice, drain and keep warm. Meanwhile, slice the chicken breast in half lengthways so that you have two thin steaks.

2. Combine the breadcrumbs and cheese. Dip the chicken in the flour, followed by the egg and then the cheese and breadcrumb mix.

3. Heat the oil in a frying pan over a moderate heat. Once hot, fry the chicken escalopes for 8-10 minutes on each side until golden.

4. Cook the mixed vegetables in a pan of boiling water until soft, then mix with the rice. Serve together with the cooked chicken.

Red rice risotto

SERVES: 2 | PREP TIME: 15 MINUTES | COOKING TIME: 45 MINUTES

INGREDIENTS

1 tbsp olive oil

1 onion, diced

1 clove of garlic, chopped

2 sticks of celery, sliced

250 g / 9 oz / 1 ¼ cups red rice

500 ml / 17 fl. oz / 2 cups vegetable stock

200 g / 7 oz green (string) beans

1 tbsp butter

50 g / 1 ¾ oz / ½ cup grated parmesan

handful of basil leaves

METHOD

1. Heat the oil in a large heavy bottomed pan, then sauté the onions for 5–6 minutes until soft and translucent. Add the garlic and celery and cook for a further minute.

2. Add the rice to the pan and mix through the onions for a couple of minutes. Gradually add the stock to the pan, covering the pan after each addition. Leave for 10 minutes each time to absorb the liquid.

3. Cook the beans in salted boiling water for 10 minutes. Drain and add to the rice.

4. Once the rice is tender, stir through the butter and parmesan. Season to taste.

5. Serve in bowls with basil leaves as garnish.

Ham and cheese quiche

SERVES: 4-6 | PREP TIME: 20 MINUTES | COOKING TIME: 45 MINUTES

INGREDIENTS

2 large potatoes, peeled and cubed

2 tbsp olive oil

1 onion, diced

1 clove of garlic, chopped

150 g / 5 ¼ oz ham, diced

1 tbsp plain (all-purpose) flour

200 ml / 7 fl. oz / ¾ cup milk

6 eggs, beaten

150 g / 5 ¼ oz / 1 ½ cups Cheddar cheese, grated

handful of fresh basil

METHOD

1. Preheat the oven to 180°C (160°C fan) / 350F / gas 4.

2. Boil the potatoes in a pan of salted water for 10 minutes until tender but still firm enough to hold their shape. Drain and set aside.

3. Heat the oil in an ovenproof frying pan over a medium heat. Cook the onions for 4-6 minutes until softened. Add the garlic and cook for a further minute, then add the potatoes and ham and mix through.

4. Whisk together the flour, milk and eggs. Mix through the cheese and season to taste. Pour into the frying pan, transfer to the oven and bake for 45 minutes until golden and puffed up.

5. Transfer to a serving board and scatter the basil.

74

Chicken and avocado salad

SERVES: 1 | PREP TIME: 5 MINUTES | COOKING TIME: 12 MINUTES

INGREDIENTS

1 x 125 g / 4 ½ oz skinless chicken breast

2 tbsp olive oil

1 large handful mixed salad leaves

½ avocado, peeled and stoned

2 cherry tomatoes, halved

1 tbsp lemon juice

½ tsp caster (superfine) sugar

½ tsp mustard

METHOD

1. Heat a griddle pan until smoking hot. Brush the chicken with 1 tablespoon of the oil and season all over with salt and pepper.

2. Griddle the chicken for 12 minutes, turning every 3 minutes or until it's cooked through and nicely marked. Cut the chicken across into three big pieces.

3. Arrange the lettuce leaves in a bowl and top with the avocado, tomatoes and chicken.

4. Whisk the rest of the oil with the lemon juice, sugar and mustard and season with salt and pepper. Drizzle it over the salad and serve immediately.

75

Cheese and steak panini

SERVES: 1 | PREP TIME: 10 MINUTES | COOKING TIME: 10 MINUTES

INGREDIENTS

1 thin minute steak

2 tbsp olive oil

½ small onion, thinly sliced

½ green pepper, thinly sliced

1 focaccia roll, halved horizontally

2 slices Provolone cheese

METHOD

1. Lay the steak between two sheets of cling film and use a rolling pin or wine bottle to gently bash it out to 3 mm thick. Cut into sections to make it easier to fry.

2. Heat a frying pan until smoking hot. Brush the steak with half of the oil and season with salt and pepper. Fry for 30 seconds on each side, then transfer to a plate.

3. Reduce the heat of the frying pan and add the rest of the oil with the onion and green pepper. Stir-fry for 5 minutes.

4. Preheat a panini press or sandwich toaster. Arrange the steak on the base of the roll and top with the peppers and onions. Lay the cheese on top and cover with the roll tops.

5. Toast the sandwich for 3 minutes or until the bread is golden brown and the cheese has melted. Cut in half and serve immediately.

Pepperoni, olive and onion pizza

MAKES: 1 | PREP TIME: 2 HOURS | COOKING TIME: 12 MINUTES

INGREDIENTS

150 g / 5 ½ oz / 1 cup strong white bread flour, plus extra for dusting

½ tsp easy blend dried yeast

½ tsp fine sea salt

½ tbsp olive oil

2 tbsp tomato pizza sauce

125 g / 4 ½ oz / 1 ball mozzarella, sliced

10 slices pepperoni

¼ red onion, sliced

4 black olives, stoned and sliced

¼ tsp herbes de Provence

METHOD

1. Mix together the flour, yeast and salt and stir the oil into 100 ml of warm water. Stir the liquid into the dry ingredients then knead on a lightly oiled surface for 10 minutes or until smooth and elastic.

2. Leave the dough to rest covered with oiled cling film for 1–2 hours until doubled in size.

3. Preheat the oven to 240°C (220°C fan) / 475F / gas 9 and grease a large baking tray.

4. Knead the dough for 2 more minutes then roll it out into a rough circle.

5. Transfer the base to the prepared tray and spread with tomato pizza sauce.

6. Arrange the cheese, pepperoni, onion and olives on top and sprinkle with herbes de Provence.

7. Bake for 12 minutes or until the base is cooked through underneath.

8. Serve immediately.

Creamy chicken and rice

SERVES: 2-4 | PREP TIME: 15 MINUTES | COOKING TIME: 30 MINUTES

INGREDIENTS

200 g / 7 oz / 1 cup long grain rice

2 tbsp olive oil

1 onion, diced

1 clove of garlic, chopped

3 carrots, diced

300 g / 10 ½ oz chicken breast, diced

1 tbsp plain (all-purpose) flour

250 ml / 9 fl. oz / 1 cup milk

50 g / 1 ¾ oz / ½ cup parmesan cheese, grated

METHOD

1. Cook the rice and set aside.

2. Heat the oil in a large heavy bottomed pan over a moderate heat and cook the onion for 3-5 minutes until soft. Add the garlic and carrots and cook for a further 2–3 minutes.

3. Add the chicken and brown the meat. Stir through the flour and cook for 2 minutes.

4. Gradually add the milk, stirring continuously until you have a thick and creamy sauce. Mix through the cheese and season. Leave to simmer for 8-10 minutes until the chicken is cooked through.

5. Mix the rice through the chicken and serve in bowls.

Chicken curry

SERVES: 4 | PREP TIME: 5 MINUTES | COOKING TIME: 45 MINUTES

INGREDIENTS

2 tbsp sunflower oil

1 onion, finely chopped

1 tbsp fresh root ginger, grated

3 cloves of garlic, crushed

skinless, boneless chicken thighs, cut into chunks

1 tbsp curry powder

400 g / 14 oz / 2 cups canned tomatoes, chopped

200 ml/ 7 fl. oz / ¾ cup coconut milk

2 tbsp mango chutney

1 small bunch coriander, chopped

METHOD

1. Heat the oil in a large saucepan and fry the onion for 8 minutes stirring occasionally. Add the ginger and garlic and stir-fry for a further 2 minutes.

2. Add the chicken and cook for 4 minutes, stirring occasionally, until it starts to colour on the outside. Sprinkle over the curry powder and continue to cook for 1 minute.

3. Add the tomatoes, coconut milk and mango chutney and bring to a gentle simmer. Add water if the sauce doesn't cover the chicken.

4. Cook the curry for 30 minutes, stirring occasionally, until the chicken is tender and the sauce has thickened.

Tuna niçoise

SERVES: 2 | PREP TIME: 15 MINUTES | COOKING TIME: 10 MINUTES

INGREDIENTS

1 egg

100 g / 3 ½ oz green (string) beans, trimmed

250 g / 9 oz canned tuna, drained

50 g / 1 ¾ oz / ⅓ cup black olives

100 g / 3 ½ oz mixed salad leaves, washed

½ red onion, sliced

50 g / 1 ¾ oz cherry tomatoes, halved

2 tbsp olive oil

1 clove of garlic, minced

1 tsp Dijon mustard

1 lemon, juiced

METHOD

1. Place the egg into a saucepan of cold water. Heat until boiling and then leave for 3-4 minutes before draining. Refill the pan with cold water to stop the egg cooking further. Once cold enough to handle, peel and half the egg.

2. Cook the beans in a pan of salted boiling water for 6–8 minutes until tender, drain and set aside.

3. Assemble the salad by arranging the egg, tuna and vegetables on a plate or in a bowl.

4. Place the oil, garlic, mustard and lemon in a sealable jar or contained. Shake well to combine before drizzling over the salad.

Cheesy baked mushrooms

SERVES: 2 | PREP TIME: 10 MINUTES | COOKING TIME: 25 MINUTES

INGREDIENTS

4 portabello mushrooms, stalks removed

5 button mushrooms, stalks removed

2 tbsp olive oil

2 tbsp pesto

4 cherry tomatoes, quartered

125 g / 4 ½ oz / 1 ball mozzarella, chopped

2 tbsp Gruyère cheese, grated

2 tbsp flat leaf parsley, finely chopped, plus a few
leaves to garnish

METHOD

1. Preheat the oven to 200°C (180°C fan) /
   400F / gas 6.

2. Brush the mushrooms with oil and arrange
   them open-side-up in a greaseproof paper
   lined baking dish.

3. Fill the portabello mushrooms with pesto
   and the button mushrooms with tomato.
   Mix the mozzarella with the Gruyère and
   parsley and sprinkle over the top.

4. Bake the mushrooms for 25 minutes or until
   tender to the point of a knife.

5. Season with black pepper and serve
   immediately.

Baked potatoes with chilli con carne

SERVES: 6 | PREP TIME: 5 MINUTES | COOKING TIME: 40 MINUTES

INGREDIENTS

2 tbsp olive oil

1 onion, finely chopped

2 cloves of garlic, crushed

½ tsp cayenne pepper

450 g / 1 lb / 3 cups minced beef

400 g / 14 oz / 2 cups canned tomatoes, chopped

200 ml / 7 fl. oz / ¾ cup beef stock

400 g / 14 oz / 2 cups canned kidney beans, drained

6 baking potatoes

100 ml / 3 ½ fl. oz / ½ cup soured cream

100 g / 3 ½ oz / 1 cup Double Gloucester cheese, grated

4 spring onions (scallions), chopped

METHOD

1. Preheat the oven to 220°C (200°C fan) / 425F / gas 7.

2. Heat the oil in a large saucepan and fry the onion for 5 minutes, stirring occasionally. Add the garlic and cayenne and cook for 2 minutes, then add the mince.

3. Fry the mince until it starts to brown then add the chopped tomatoes, stock and kidney beans and bring to a gentle simmer. Cook the chilli con carne for 30 minutes, stirring occasionally, until the mince is tender and the sauce has thickened a little.

4. Meanwhile, prick the potatoes and microwave for 5 minutes. Transfer the potatoes to the oven and bake for 30 minutes.

5. Taste the chilli for seasoning and add salt and freshly ground black pepper as necessary. Cut open the potatoes and fill with chilli con carne. Add a dollop of soured cream to each one and sprinkle with cheese and spring onions before serving.

Pad thai

SERVES: 4 | PREP TIME: 15 MINUTES | COOKING TIME: 10 MINUTES

INGREDIENTS

200 g / 7 oz dried Pho or Pad Thai rice noodles

3 tbsp vegetable oil

2 large eggs, beaten

2 cloves garlic, finely chopped

1 tbsp root ginger, julienned

3 spring onions (scallions), chopped

200 g / 7 oz / 1 ⅓ cups raw prawns, peeled
with tails left intact

2 tbsp oyster sauce

1 tbsp light soy sauce

2 limes, 1 juiced, 1 cut into 8 pieces

2 tsp caster (superfine) sugar

3 tbsp salted peanuts, finely chopped

1 tsp chilli (chili) flakes

sliced chilli and parsley leaves to garnish

METHOD

1. Put the rice noodles into a heatproof bowl,
   cover with boiling water and leave to soften
   for 15 minutes.

2. Heat half the oil in a large wok then pour in
   the egg. Cook for 1 minute or until almost set,
   then flip it over and cook the other side. Slide
   it onto a chopping board and cut into
   small pieces.

3. Add the rest of the oil to the wok and fry the
   garlic, ginger and spring onions for
   30 seconds.

4. Add the prawns and stir fry for 2 minutes or
   until they just turn opaque.

5. Stir the oyster sauce, soy, lime juice and
   sugar together and add it to the wok,
   followed by the drained noodles.

6. Stir-fry for 1 more minute then stir in the
   peanuts and divide between four
   warm bowls.

7. Top each bowl with a couple of chunks of
   lime and a sprinkle of chilli flakes, then
   garnish with chilli and parsley.

Tagliatelle with chicken and pesto

SERVES: 4 | PREP TIME: 15 MINUTES | COOKING TIME: 5 MINUTES

INGREDIENTS

½ clove of garlic

1 ½ tbsp pine nuts, toasted

50 g / 1 ¾ oz / 2 cups basil leaves, plus extra to garnish

25 g Pecorino, finely grated

200 ml / 7 fl. oz / ¾ cup extra virgin olive oil

2 skinless chicken breasts, sliced

500 g / 1 lb 1 ¾ oz fresh egg tagliatelle pasta

METHOD

1. For the pesto, crush the garlic with a pinch of salt in a large pestle and mortar. Add the pine nuts and pound until broken up, then gradually add the basil and pound until well pulped. Stir in the cheese and all but 2 tablespoons of the olive oil.

2. Heat the remaining oil in a frying pan. Fry the chicken on a medium heat for until cooked through and golden brown.

3. Cook the pasta until al dente. Drain and toss with the pesto and chicken.

4. Divide between four warm bowls and serve immediately, garnished with basil.

Steak and salad flatbreads

SERVES: 2 | PREP TIME: 5 MINUTES | COOKING TIME: 8 MINUTES

INGREDIENTS

1 small rump steak

2 flatbreads

1 tsp mustard

1 ½ tbsp mayonnaise

4 little gem lettuce leaves

½ red pepper, sliced

2 spring onions (scallions), sliced

2 tbsp canned sweetcorn

METHOD

1. Heat a frying pan until smoking hot. Season the steak generously with salt and pepper, then cook for 4 minutes on each side. Transfer to a plate and leave to rest while you assemble the flatbreads.

2. Warm the flatbreads in the frying pan for 20 seconds on each side.

3. Mix the mustard with the mayonnaise and spread thinly over the flatbreads. Top with lettuce, pepper, spring onion and sweetcorn.

4. Thinly slice the steak and divide between the flatbreads, then roll up and serve.

89

Leek and mushroom quiche

SERVES: 6 | PREP TIME: 1 HOUR | COOKING TIME: 40 MINUTES

INGREDIENTS

2 tbsp butter

1 large leek, thinly sliced

2 cloves of garlic, sliced

225 g / 8 oz / 3 cups mixed mushrooms, chopped

3 large eggs, beaten

225 ml / 8 fl. oz / ¾ cup double (heavy)cream

75 g / 2 ½ oz / ½ cup Gruyère, grated

basil and parsley, to garnish

FOR THE PASTRY:

110 g / 4 oz / ½ cup butter, cubed and chilled

225 g / 8 oz / 1 ½ cups plain (all-purpose) flour

METHOD

1. To make the pastry, rub the butter into the flour until the mixture resembles fine breadcrumbs. Stir in just enough cold water to bring the pastry together into a pliable dough, then chill for 30 minutes.

2. Preheat the oven to 200°C (180°C fan) / 400F / gas 6.

3. Roll out the pastry and use it to line a 23 cm (9 in) loose-bottomed tart tin. Prick it with a fork, line with baking or greaseproof paper and fill with baking beans. Bake for 10 minutes, then remove the paper and beans and cook for 5 minutes or until crisp.

4. Lower the oven to 150°C (130°C fan) / 300F / gas 2. Heat the butter in a large sauté pan and fry the leek for 5 minutes. Add the garlic and mushrooms and sauté for 10 minutes.

5. Whisk the eggs with the double cream then stir in the vegetables. Season generously with salt and pepper.

6. Pour the filling into the pastry case and scatter the cheese on top.

7. Bake for 40 minutes or until just set in the centre. Leave the quiche to cool to room temperature, then garnish with basil and parsley and serve.

Red lentil flan

SERVES: 6-8 | PREP TIME: 30 MINUTES | COOKING TIME: 1 HOUR

INGREDIENTS

300 g / 10 ½ oz / 2 cups wholemeal plain
(all-purpose) flour

150 g / 5 ¼ oz / ⅔ cup butter, cut into cubes

2 tbsp milk

200 g / 7 oz red lentils

500 ml / 17 fl. oz / 2 cups vegetable stock

1 tbsp olive oil

1 onion, diced

1 red pepper, diced

1 clove of garlic, minced

1 tbsp tomato puree

1 tsp chilli (chili) flakes

handful of flat leaf parsley, chopped

METHOD

1. Preheat the oven to 180°C (160°C fan) / 350F / gas 4 and lightly grease a flan tin.

2. Place the flour into a bowl and rub in the butter with your fingertips until the mixture resembles fine breadcrumbs. Add the milk a little at a time and mix until a smooth dough forms. Roll into a bowl and wrap with cling film before placing into the refrigerator to rest.

3. Place the lentils into a saucepan and cover with the stock. Cook for 15–20 minutes until tender. Drain and set aside.

4. Heat the oil in a frying pan over a moderate heat. Add the onions and pepper and cook for 5–6 minutes until softened. Stir through the garlic and tomato puree.

5. Add the chilli flakes and lentil and mix through until fully combined. Remove from the heat and season with salt and black pepper to taste.

6. Remove the pastry from the refrigerator and roll out to roughly 2mm thickness. Press into the flan tin and press into the edges with your finger. Lightly prick the base with a fork.

7. Fill the flan with the lentil mixture before baking in the oven for 30 minutes until crisp and golden.

8. Remove and allow to cool a little before scattering over the parsley and serving.

Macaroni cheese

SERVES: 4 | PREP TIME: 20 MINUTES | COOKING TIME: 30 MINUTES

●●●●●●●●●●●●●●●●●●●●●●●●●

INGREDIENTS

400 g / 14 oz / 4 cups dried macaroni

2 tbsp butter

2 tbsp plain (all-purpose) flour

600 ml / 1 pint / 2 ½ cups milk

150 g / 5 ½ oz / 1 ½ cup Cheddar cheese, grated

2 tbsp dried breadcrumbs

METHOD

1. Preheat the oven to 180°C (160°C fan) / 350F / gas 4.

2. Cook the macaroni in boiling, salted water for 10 minutes or until almost cooked. Drain well.

3. Meanwhile, put the butter, flour and milk in a saucepan. Cook the sauce over a low heat, stirring constantly, until the mixture bubbles and thickens. Take the pan off the heat and stir in two thirds of the cheese. Season to taste with salt and pepper.

4. Stir the macaroni into the cheese sauce and scrape it into a baking dish.

5. Sprinkle over the remaining cheese and the breadcrumbs, then bake for 30 minutes or until the top is golden brown and the pasta is cooked.

Aubergine and halloumi burgers

SERVES: 4 | PREP TIME: 25 MINUTES | COOKING TIME: 20 MINUTES

INGREDIENTS

1 small aubergine (eggplant), cut into 4 mm slices

2 small courgettes (zucchini), cut lengthways into 4 mm slices

50 ml / 1 ¾ fl. oz / ¼ cup olive oil

4 sesame burger buns, halved horizontally

250 g / 9 oz / 1 block halloumi, cut horizontally into 4 slices

2 tbsp mayonnaise

4 lettuce leaves

METHOD

1. Lay out the sliced vegetables and sprinkle both sides with salt and pepper. Leave to sweat for 15 minutes, then blot dry.

2. Brush the vegetables with the oil and cook on a hot griddle pan until pleasingly marked. Keep warm in an oven on a low heat.

3. Toast the cut side of the buns in the same way, set aside and grill the halloumi.

4. Spread the buns with mayonnaise, then layer the lettuce, vegetables and halloumi. Top the buns and serve immediately.

95

Tandoori chicken skewers

SERVES: 2 | PREP TIME: 15 MINUTES | MARINATE TIME: 1 HOUR
COOKING TIME: 8 MINUTES

••••••••••••••••••••••••••

INGREDIENTS

50 ml / 1 ¾ fl. oz / ¼ cup natural yogurt

1 clove of garlic, crushed

1 tsp curry powder

2 tsp mango chutney

4 skinless, boneless chicken thighs,
cut into large chunks

2 tbsp coriander (cilantro) leaves, chopped

lemon wedges, to serve

METHOD

1. Mix the yogurt with the garlic, curry powder
   and chutney and massage it into the chicken.

2. Leave to marinate for at least 1 hour in the fridge.

3. Preheat the grill to its highest setting. Thread
   the chicken pieces onto six metal skewers.

4. Cook the skewers under the grill for
   4 minutes on each side, or until the
   chicken is cooked through.

5. Sprinkle with coriander and serve immediately
   with lemon wedges for squeezing over.

Chilli con carne

SERVES: 4 | PREP TIME: 20 MINUTES | COOKING TIME: 1 HOUR

INGREDIENTS

2 tbsp olive oil
2 onions, diced
2 red peppers, deseeded and sliced
2 cloves of garlic, minced
1 red chilli (chili), deseeded finely chopped
1 tsp cumin
1 tsp coriander (cilantro)
1 tsp smoked paprika
2 tsp chilli (chili) powder
500 g / 1 lb 1 oz beef mince
400 g / 14 oz chopped tomatoes, canned
400 g / 14 oz canned kidney beans, drained

METHOD

1. In a large pan heat the oil over a medium high heat. Add the onions and peppers and fry for around 5 minutes until soft and the onions are translucent.

2. Add the garlic and chilli, frying for a minute before adding the spices and beef mince. Cook for a further 3-4 minutes until browned, before adding the tomatoes. Fill the tomato can with water and add this to the pan. Increase the heat until boiling and then turn down to a simmer.

3. Leave on a simmer for up to an hour, adding the kidney beans to the pan after 30 minutes. Check the seasoning, adding salt and black pepper to taste.

4. Serve the chilli in bowls with boiled rice, tortilla chips or bread.

Aubergine and spinach bake

SERVES: 2 | PREP TIME: 20 MINUTES | COOKING TIME: 40 MINUTES

INGREDIENTS

2 large aubergines (eggplant), sliced lengthways

2 tbsp olive oil

200 g / 7 oz spinach, washed

250 g / 9 oz ricotta

2 cloves of garlic, minced

1 lemon, juiced

60 g / 2 oz / ½ cup parmesan, grated

50 g / 1 ¾ oz / ½ cup walnuts, chopped

METHOD

1. Preheat the oven to 180°C (160°C fan) / 350F / gas 4.

2. Place a griddle pan onto a medium high heat. Brush the aubergine slices with the oil and place onto the hot griddle pan and cook for 2–3 minutes on each side until charred and tender.

3. Place the spinach into a colander over the sink and pour over a kettle of hot water to wilt. Once cool enough to handle, squeeze out as much moisture as possible.

4. Mix the spinach with the ricotta, garlic and lemon juice before seasoning with salt and black pepper.

5. Place a layer of aubergine in the bottom of an ovenproof dish and top with a layer of the spinach mixture. Repeat until all the ingredients have been used, finishing with a layer of spinach.

6. Top with the grated parmesan and scatter over the nuts.

7. Bake in the oven for 30 minutes until set and the top has turned golden brown.

Chicken stew with mash

SERVES: 2-4 | PREP TIME: 15 MINUTES | COOKING TIME: 1 HOUR

INGREDIENTS

2 tbsp olive oil

800 g / 1 lb 12 oz chicken thighs, skinless and boneless

1 onion, diced

2 cloves of garlic, minced

200 g / 7 oz chestnut mushrooms, chopped

1 tbsp tomato puree

1 tsp dried tarragon

350 ml / 11 ¾ fl. oz / 1 ½ cups chicken stock

150 ml / 5 ¼ fl. oz / ⅔ cup double (heavy) cream

1 tbsp Dijon mustard

1 lemon, juiced

400 g / 14 oz potatoes, peeled and diced

100 g / 3 ½ oz / ½ cup butter

METHOD

1. Preheat the oven to 180°C (160°C fan) / 350F / gas 4.

2. Heat the oil in a large casserole or ovenproof pan over a medium heat. Roughly chop the chicken and add to the pan and brown in the oil, in batches if necessary. Remove with a slotted spoon and set aside.

3. Add the onion to the pan and cook for 4–5 minutes until softened. Add the garlic and mushrooms and cook for a further 5–7 minutes at which point the mushrooms will have released their liquid.

4. Mix through the tomato puree and tarragon, pour in the stock and cream before stirring through the mustard and lemon juice. Heat until boiling and then reduce to a simmer. Return the chicken to the pan, cover and transfer to the oven for 45 minutes.

5. Once the chicken is in the oven, cook the potatoes in a pan of salted boiling water for 20-25 minutes until tender. Drain thoroughly before returning to the pan to steam dry.

6. Mash the potatoes with the butter until smooth, season with salt and black pepper.

7. Check the seasoning for the stew adding salt and black pepper as required. Serve with the mashed potato.

Chicken tacos

SERVES: 2-4 | PREP TIME: 15 MINUTES | COOKING TIME: 20 MINUTES

INGREDIENTS

4 mini tortillas
300 g / 10 ½ oz chicken thighs, skinless and boneless
1 tsp cumin
1 tsp coriander (cilantro)
1 tsp paprika
1 tbsp vegetable oil
200 g / 7 oz refried beans
½ red onion, sliced
2 red chillies (chili), sliced
¼ lettuce, leaves washed
100 g / 3 ½ oz / 1 cup Cheddar cheese, grated

METHOD

1. Preheat the oven to 180°C (160°C fan) / 350F / gas 4.

2. Turn a muffin tin upside down and place the tortillas in the gaps to form a taco. Bake in the oven for 10 minutes until they hold their shape.

3. Slice the chicken into strips and put in a bowl with the cumin, coriander and paprika. Toss the chicken in the spices to coat and season to taste.

4. Heat the oil in a non-stick frying pan over a moderate heat. Once hot, cook the chicken and for 8–10 minutes until browned. Add the beans and cook together for a further 10 minutes. Add a splash of water if the pan dries out.

5. Serve the mixture inside the taco shells and top with the rest of the ingredients.

Buckwheat risotto with lamb

SERVES: 2 | PREP TIME: 15 MINUTES | COOKING TIME: 30 MINUTES

INGREDIENTS

2 tbsp butter

1 tsp olive oil

1 onion, diced

1 clove of garlic, chopped

150 g / 5 ¼ oz chestnut mushrooms, sliced

150 g / 5 ¼ oz buckwheat groats

500 ml / 17 fl. oz / 2 cups vegetable stock, warmed

50 g / 1 ¾ oz / ½ cup Parmesan, grated

300 g / 10 ½ oz lamb steaks

1 orange, zest only

handful of flat leaf parsley, chopped

METHOD

1. Heat half the butter and the oil in a heavy bottomed pan over a medium heat. Cook the onion for 4-5 minutes until softened. Add the garlic and mushrooms and cook for a further 5 minutes until the mushrooms colour slightly.

2. Add the buckwheat and stir through for a couple of minutes. Gradually add the stock at a simmer. Allow the liquid to absorb before adding more. Once tender, mix through the Parmesan.

3. As the risotto is cooking, heat the remaining butter in a frying pan. Season the lamb and add to the pan once the butter is frothy. Cook for 12–15 minutes, depending on your preference. Remove and slice.

4. Mix the lamb into the risotto along with the orange zest and parsley before serving.

Rustic potato and beef soup

SERVES: 2-4 | PREP TIME: 15 MINUTES | COOKING TIME: 45 MINUTES

INGREDIENTS

2 tbsp olive oil

500 g / 1 lb 1 oz braising beef, diced

1 onion, roughly chopped

4 carrots, sliced

500 ml / 17 fl. oz / 2 cups beef stock

400 g / 14 oz canned chopped tomatoes

4 potatoes, cubed

small bunch of flat leaf parsley

METHOD

1. Heat the oil in a heavy bottomed casserole pan over a high heat. Cook the beef for 2 minutes to brown before removing with a slotted spoon.

2. Add the onion and carrots to the pan and fry for 3–5 minutes until starting to brown at the edges. Return the beef and any juices that have collected and stir through.

3. Pour the stock and tomatoes into the pan and add the potatoes and half the parsley. Increase the heat until boiling before turning down to a simmer and seasoning with salt and black pepper.

4. Cook for 40 minutes until the beef is soft and vegetables are tender. Serve in bowls with crusty bread and the remaining parsley as a garnish.

Spicy chicken spaghetti

SERVES: 1 | PREP TIME: 10 MINUTES | COOKING TIME: 20 MINUTES

INGREDIENTS

80 g / 2 ¾ oz spaghetti

1 chicken breast, diced

1 tsp paprika

1 tsp cayenne

½ lemon, juiced

1 tbsp olive oil

1 tbsp tomato puree

handful of flat leaf parlsey, chopped

METHOD

1. Place the spaghetti into a pan of salted boiling water and cook as per the packet instructions. Drain, reserving some of the liquid as required.

2. Mix the chicken with the paprika, cayenne and lemon juice. Season with salt and black pepper.

3. Heat the oil in a frying pan over a medium heat. Add the chicken and cook for 18-20 minutes, stirring through the tomato puree once the meat has browned. Add a splash of the pasta water to loosen the sauce.

4. Add the spaghetti into the pan with the chicken and mix through to coat with the sauce.

5. Serve hot with the parsley scattered over the top.

Courgette and dill frittata

SERVES: 4 | PREP TIME: 5 MINUTES | COOKING TIME: 30 MINUTES

INGREDIENTS

4 tbsp olive oil

2 shallots, thinly sliced

2 courgettes (zucchini), halved and thinly sliced

1 garlic clove, crushed

6 large eggs

1 small bunch dill, finely chopped

METHOD

1. Heat 3 tablespoons of the oil in an oven-proof frying pan and fry the shallots and courgette for 15 minutes over a low heat until softened and lightly caramelised. Add the garlic and season with salt and pepper, then cook for 2 more minutes.

2. Preheat the grill to its highest setting. Gently beat the eggs in a jug to break up the yolks then stir in the courgette mixture and dill.

3. Wipe out the frying pan with kitchen paper then heat the rest of the oil in the pan. Pour in the mixture and cook over a gentle heat for 8 minutes or until the outside has set.

4. Put the frying pan under the grill to cook the top for 3–4 minutes or until golden brown and just set.

5. Slide the frittata onto a serving plate and briefly leave to cool before serving.

Crustless potato and spinach quiche

SERVES: 4 | PREP TIME: 15 MINUTES | COOKING TIME: 1 HOUR

INGREDIENTS

2 large potatoes, peeled and sliced

2 tbsp olive oil

1 onion, diced

1 clove of garlic, chopped

100 g / 3 ½ oz spinach, washed

50 g / 1 ¾ oz / ⅓ cup peas

1 tbsp plain (all-purpose) flour

200 ml / 7 fl. oz / ¾ cup milk

6 eggs, beaten

150 g / 5 ¼ oz / 1 ½ cups Cheddar cheese, grated

handful of fresh basil, chopped

METHOD

1. Preheat the oven to 180°C (160°C fan) / 350F / gas 4 and lightly grease and ovenproof dish.

2. In a pan of salted water, boil the potatoes for 10 minutes until tender but still firm enough to hold their shape. Drain and set aside.

3. Heat the oil in a frying pan over a medium heat. Add the onions and cook for 4–6 minutes until softened. Add the garlic and cook for a further minute, before adding the spinach and peas. Cook until the spinach has wilted and any moisture has evaporated.

4. Whisk together the flour, milk and eggs. Mix through the cheese and season. Fold the fried vegetables through the mixture.

5. Arrange the potato slices in the prepared ovenproof dish. Pour over the egg mixture and bake in the hot oven for around 1 hour until golden and puffed up.

6. Serve with a scatter of basil leaves.

Pepperoni and mushroom pizza

MAKES: 2 | PREP TIME: 2 HOURS | COOKING TIME: 12 MINUTES

INGREDIENTS

200 g / 7 oz / 1 ⅓ cups strong white bread flour, plus extra for dusting

½ tsp easy blend dried yeast

2 tsp caster (superfine) sugar

1 tsp fine sea salt

1 tbsp olive oil

ml / 2 ½ fl. oz / ⅓ cup canned tomatoes, chopped

½ yellow pepper, sliced

½ red pepper, sliced

½ green pepper, sliced

1 handful pepperoni slices

2 slices ham, torn into small pieces

1 handful cherry tomatoes, halved

4 button mushrooms, sliced

1 red chilli, washed

3 sprigs of basil

METHOD

1. Mix together the flour, yeast, sugar and salt and stir the oil into 140 ml of warm water. Stir the liquid into the dry ingredients, then knead on a lightly oiled surface for 10 minutes or until smooth and elastic.

2. Leave the dough to rest covered with oiled cling film for 1–2 hours until doubled in size.

3. Preheat the oven to 240°C (220°C fan) / 475F / gas 9 and grease two large baking trays.

4. Knead the dough for 2 more minutes then divide into two pieces. Roll them out into circles. Transfer the bases to the prepared trays and spread with the canned tomato.

5. Arrange the peppers, pepperoni, ham, cherry tomatoes, mushrooms and red chilli on top.

6. Bake for 12 minutes or until the bases are cooked through underneath.

7. Cut into quarters before serving.

Vegetarian minestrone

SERVES: 4 | PREP TIME: 20 MINUTES | COOKING TIME: 45 MINUTES

INGREDIENTS

2 tbsp olive oil
1 onion, diced
2 celery sticks, chopped
2 carrots, sliced
2 cloves of garlic, chopped
1 courgette (zucchini), sliced
1 red pepper, deseeded and chopped
400 g / 14 oz canned chopped tomatoes
1 l / 35 fl. oz / 4 cups vegetable stock
150 g / 5 ¼ oz ditalini pasta
200 g / 7 oz / 1 ⅓ cup garden peas, frozen
handful basil leaves, chopped
50 g / 1 ¾ oz / ½ cup Parmesan cheese, grated

METHOD

1. Heat the oil in a large saucepan with a lid over a
   medium heat. Add the onion, celery and carrot
   and cook for 8–10 minutes until softened.

2. Add the garlic, courgette and pepper to the pan
   and continue to cook for 2–3 more minutes.

3. Add the tomatoes and stock, bring to the boil
   then replace the lid. Reduce to a simmer. Cook
   for 15 minutes until the vegetables have softened.

4. Add the pasta to the pan and cook for a further
   12–15 minutes until the pasta is cooked. Add the
   peas for the last 3–5 minutes. Season to taste and
   add more water if the soup is too thick.

5. To serve, ladle the soup into bowls and top with
   chopped basil and grated Parmesan.

Butternut squash soup

SERVES: 4 | PREP TIME: 20 MINUTES | COOKING TIME: 30 MINUTES

INGREDIENTS

1 tbsp olive oil

1 onion, diced

2 cloves of garlic, chopped

1 red chilli (chili), sliced

1 butternut squash, peeled and chopped

2 sweet potatoes, peeled and diced

1 tsp cumin

1 tsp paprika

1 tsp turmeric

750 ml / 25 fl. oz / 3 cups vegetable or chicken stock

25 g / 1 oz / ¼ cup pumpkin seeds, to garnish

METHOD

1. Heat the oil in a large saucepan over a medium heat. Add the onions and sweat for 4–5 minutes until softened. Add the garlic and chilli and stir through for 1 minute until fragrant.

2. Add the squash, sweet potatoes and mix through for a couple of minutes.

3. Pour in the stock and increase the heat until boiling. Reduce to a simmer and cover with a lid. Leave to cook for 20–25 minutes until the vegetables have softened.

4. Using a hand blender, blend the ingredients until thick and smooth. Season to taste.

5. Serve in bowls with the pumpkin seeds on top and a drizzle of olive oil.

Tagliatelle with tomato and prawns

SERVES: 4 | PREP TIME: 5 MINUTES | COOKING TIME: 20 MINUTES

INGREDIENTS

3 tbsp olive oil

1 small onion, finely chopped

2 cloves of garlic, crushed

½ tsp chilli (chili) flakes

200 g / 7 oz / 1 cup canned chopped tomatoes

400 g / 14 oz dried tagliatelle

24 raw king prawns, peeled with tails left intact

a handful of basil leaves, chopped

METHOD

1. Heat the oil in a sauté pan and fry the shallot, garlic and chilli flakes for 5 minutes. Stir in the tomatoes and cook over a low heat for 15 minutes, stirring occasionally. Season to taste with salt and pepper.

2. Meanwhile, cook the pasta in boiling, salted water until al dente.

3. Towards the end of the pasta cooking time, add the prawns to the tomato sauce, cooking and turning until both sides turn pink.

4. Drain the pasta and divide between four warm bowls. Spoon over the sauce and scatter with basil before serving.

114

Lamb stew

SERVES: 2-4 | PREP TIME: 15 MINUTES | COOKING TIME: 1 HOUR, 30 MINUTES

INGREDIENTS

2 tbsp olive oil

500 g / 1 lb 1 oz stewing lamb, diced

1 onion, roughly chopped

4 carrots, sliced

2 red peppers, deseeded and chopped

2 cloves of garlic, minced

1 tsp paprika

500 ml / 17 fl. oz / 2 cups lamb stock

4 potatoes, cubed

small bunch of flat leaf parsley

METHOD

1. Heat the oil in a heavy bottomed casserole pan
    over a high heat. Cook the lamb for 2 minutes
    to brown the meat before removing with a
    slotted spoon.

2. Add the onion, carrots and peppers to the pan
    and fry for 3–5 minutes until starting to brown
    at the edges. Add the garlic and paprika and fry
    for a further couple of minutes until fragrant.

3. Return the lamb and any juices that have been
    collected to the pan and stir through. Pour the
    stock into the pan and add the potatoes.
    Increase the heat until boiling before turning
    down to a simmer and season to taste.

4. Cook for up to 1 ½ hours until the lamb is soft
    and vegetables are tender. Serve in bowls with
    the parsley as a garnish.

115

Chicken and asparagus risotto

SERVES: 2-4 | PREP TIME: 10 MINUTES | COOKING TIME: 40 MINUTES

INGREDIENTS

3 tbsp olive oil

1 onion, diced

2 cloves garlic, minced

100 g / 3 ½ oz asparagus tips, trimmed

2 tbsp butter

300 g / 10 ½ oz / 1 ½ cup Arborio risotto rice

150 ml / 5 fl. oz / ⅔ cup white wine

500 ml / 17 fl. oz / 2 cups chicken stock, warm

300 g / 10 ½ oz leftover roast chicken, shredded

50 g / 1 ¾ oz rocket (arugula)

50 g / 1 ¾ oz / ½ cup Parmesan cheese, grated

METHOD

1. Heat the oil in a heavy bottomed pan over a medium heat. Fry onion with a pinch of salt for 3-4 minutes until soft. Add the garlic and asparagus, frying for a further 2–3 minutes.

2. Add the butter and rice, stirring to coat with the butter and oil. Turn the heat up a little and add the wine. Allow to bubble for 5 minutes or until the liquid has halved. Turn the heat down to medium.

3. Gradually add the stock, replacing the lid after each addition. Allow the liquid to absorb each time before adding more. The rice will be ready when cooked but slightly chalky. Season to taste.

4. Stir through the cooked chicken and warm through. Serve on plates with a scatter of rocket and top with Parmesan.

Chicken and pork meatballs with linguini

SERVES: 4 | PREP TIME: 30 MINUTES | COOKING TIME: 30 MINUTES

INGREDIENTS

75 ml / 2 ½ fl. oz / ⅓ cup olive oil

1 onion, finely chopped

1 clove of garlic, crushed

250 g / 9 oz / 1 ⅔ cups minced chicken

250 g / 9 oz / 1 ⅔ cups sausagemeat

50 g / 1 ¾ oz / ⅔ cup fresh white breadcrumbs

2 tbsp basil leaves, chopped, plus extra to garnish

2 tbsp Parmesan, finely grated, plus
extra to garnish

1 egg yolk

300 g / 10 ½ oz / 2 cups cherry tomatoes

400 g / 14 oz linguini pasta

METHOD

1. Preheat the oven to 200°C (180°C fan) / 400F
    / gas 6 and grease a baking dish.

2. Heat half of the oil in a frying pan and fry
    the onion for 5 minutes or until softened.
    Add the garlic and cook for 2 more minutes,
    stirring constantly, then scrape the mixture
    into a mixing bowl and leave to cool.

3. Add the chicken mince, sausagemeat,
    breadcrumbs, basil, Parmesan and egg yolk.
    Season with salt and pepper, then mix well
    and shape into 16 meatballs.

4. Mingle the meatballs and tomatoes in the
    baking dish and drizzle with the rest of the
    oil. Bake for 20 minutes or until the
    meatballs are cooked through and the
    tomatoes have burst.

5. Meanwhile, boil the pasta in salted water
    until al dente. Drain the pasta and divide
    between four warm bowls.

6. Spoon over the meatballs and tomatoes and
    garnish with Parmesan and basil.

119

Stuffed aubergine

SERVES: 1 | PREP TIME: 15 MINUTES | COOKING TIME: 40 MINUTES

INGREDIENTS

1 aubergine (eggplant)

1 tbsp olive oil

½ onion, diced

½ red pepper, diced

½ green pepper, diced

1 clove of garlic, chopped

1 tsp turmeric

1 tsp paprika

50 g / 1 ¾ oz / ¼ cup rice, cooked

50 g / 1 ¾ oz Greek yogurt

1 egg, beaten

1 tsp cumin

½ lemon, juiced

basil leaves to garnish

METHOD

1. Preheat the oven to 180°C (160°C fan) / 350F / gas 4.

2. Cut the aubergine in half and scoop out the flesh before cutting into cubes.

3. Heat the oil in a frying pan over a moderate heat. Add the onion and peppers and cook for 5–6 minutes until softened.

4. Add the aubergine, garlic and spices to the pan and cook for a further minute until fragrant. Stir the rice through the vegetables, remove from the heat and season.

5. Place the aubergine halves into an ovenproof dish. Spoon the vegetables and rice filling into the aubergine.

6. Whisk together the yogurt, egg, cumin and lemon juice. Spoon on top of the aubergine and bake in the oven for 30 minutes.

7. Remove and serve with fresh basil to garnish.

Squash and chickpea stew

SERVES: 4 | PREP TIME: 5 MINUTES | COOKING TIME: 35 MINUTES

INGREDIENTS

50 ml / 1 ¾ fl. oz / ¼ cup olive oil

1 onion, finely chopped

1 celery stick, finely chopped

2 carrots, diced

2 cloves of garlic, finely chopped

1 tsp ground cumin

1 tsp smoked paprika

2 acorn squashes, peeled, deseeded and diced
(or 1 small butternut squash)

400 g / 14 oz / 2 cups canned tomatoes, chopped

500 ml / 17 ½ fl. oz / 2 cups vegetable stock

50 g / 1 ¾ oz / ¼ cup mixed brown and wild rice

400 g / 14 oz / 2 cups canned chickpeas (garbanzo
beans), drained

chives, to garnish

METHOD

1. Heat the oil in a large saucepan and fry the
   onion, celery, carrot and garlic for 5 minutes
   to soften without colouring.

2. Add the spices and squash to the pan and stir
   to coat in the oil, then add the tomatoes,
   stock, rice and chickpeas.

3. Simmer for 25 minutes or until the squash
   and rice are tender.

4. Season to taste with salt and pepper, then
   ladle into four warm bowls and serve
   garnished with chives.

Cook's Corner

Student Cookbook

Sides and snacks

Fennel and chilli sausage rolls

MAKES: 12 | PREP TIME: 15 MINUTES | COOKING TIME: 25 MINUTES

INGREDIENTS

350 g / 12 oz / 2 cups sausagemeat

1 clove of garlic, crushed

1 tsp chilli (chili) flakes

1 ½ tbsp fennel seeds

500 g / 1 lb 2 oz all-butter puff pastry

1 egg, beaten

METHOD

1. Preheat the oven to 230°C (210°C fan) / 450F / gas 8.

2. Mix the sausagemeat with the garlic, chilli flakes and 1 tsp of the fennel seeds.

3. Roll out the pastry on a lightly floured surface into a large rectangle and cut in half lengthways.

4. Shape the sausagemeat into two long sausages the length of the pastry strips, then fold over the pastry to enclose.

5. Seal the edge with beaten egg and roll so that the join is underneath. Cut each long roll into six pieces and transfer to a baking tray lined with greaseproof paper.

6. Brush the tops with beaten egg and sprinkle with the rest of the fennel seeds, then bake for 25 minutes or until golden brown and cooked through.

White cob loaves

MAKES: 2 LOAVES | PREP TIME: 3 HOURS | COOKING TIME: 40 MINUTES

INGREDIENTS

800 g / 1 lb 12 oz / 5 ⅓ cups strong white bread flour,
plus extra for dusting

2 tsp easy blend dried yeast

1 tbsp caster (superfine) sugar

2 tsp fine sea salt

2 tbsp butter, melted

METHOD

1. Mix together the flour, yeast, sugar and salt.
   Stir the butter into 560 ml of warm water
   then stir it into the dry ingredients.

2. Knead the mixture on a lightly oiled surface
   for 10 minutes or until smooth and elastic.
   Leave the dough to rest in an oiled bowl,
   covered with oiled cling film, for 1-2 hours or
   until doubled in size.

3. Knead for 2 minutes then divide in half.
   Shape into round loaves and transfer to two
   oiled baking trays. Cover with oiled
   cling film and leave to prove for 1 hour or
   until doubled in size.

4. Meanwhile, preheat the oven to 220°C
   (200°C fan) / 425F / gas 7.

5. Make decorative slashes in the top of the
   loaves with a sharp knife or scalpel and
   sprinkle with flour.

6. Bake for 40 minutes or until the loaves sound
   hollow when you tap them underneath.

7. Transfer to a wire rack and leave to cool
   completely before cutting.

Hummus

SERVES: 4 | PREPARATION TIME: 5 MINUTES

INGREDIENTS

400 g / 14 oz / 2 ⅔ cups canned chickpeas
(garbanzo beans), drained

90 ml / 3 fl. oz / ⅔ cup olive oil, plus extra to garnish

1 tbsp tahini paste

1 lemon, juiced

1 clove of garlic, crushed

1 pinch smoked paprika

METHOD

1. Put the chickpeas in a food processor with the oil, tahini, lemon juice and garlic.

2. Blend to a smooth puree, then season to taste with salt and pepper.

3. Spoon into a bowl and garnish with a sprinkle of smoked paprika and an extra drizzle of oil.

Tomato and sweetcorn salsa

SERVES: 6 | PREP TIME: 5 MINUTES | COOKING TIME: 20 MINUTES

INGREDIENTS

2 tbsp olive oil

1 onion, finely chopped

2 cloves of garlic, crushed

400 g / 14 oz / 2 cups canned tomatoes, chopped

200 g / 7 oz / 1 cup canned sweetcorn, drained

1 tsp caster (superfine) sugar

2 tbsp pickled jalapeños, finely chopped

1 tbsp coriander (cilantro), chopped

tortilla chips, to serve

METHOD

1. Heat the oil in a saucepan and fry the onion for 5 minutes, stirring occasionally. Add the garlic and stir-fry for 2 more minutes.

2. Add the tomatoes and sweetcorn and simmer for 10 minutes, then stir in the sugar and jalapeños.

3. Season to taste with salt and pepper, then leave to cool and chill in the fridge.

4. Scatter the salsa with coriander before serving with tortilla chips on the side.

Roasted butternut squash

MAKES: 6 | PREP TIME: 5 MINUTES | COOKING TIME: 45 MINUTES

INGREDIENTS

3 small butternut squashes, halved and deseeded

50 ml / 1 ¾ fl. oz / ¼ cup olive oil

METHOD

1. Preheat the oven to 200°C (180°C fan) / 400F / gas 6 and line a baking tray with greaseproof paper.

2. Arrange the squash halves cut side up on the baking tray and drizzle with oil. Season generously with salt and pepper.

3. Roast the squash for 45 minutes or until a skewer slides easily into the thickest part.

Oven-baked beetroot crisps

ERVES: 4 | PREP TIME: 15 MINUTES | COOKING TIME: 1 HOUR, 30 MINUTES

INGREDIENTS

4 medium beetroot, peeled

50 ml / 1 ¾ fl. oz / ¼ cup olive oil

coarse sea salt

METHOD

1. Preheat the oven to 140°C (120°C fan) / 275F / gas 1 and line two large baking trays with greaseproof paper.

2. Cut the beetroot into 3 mm slices with a mandolin or a food processor with a slicing attachment. Tip them into a large bowl and drizzle with the oil, then massage it in as evenly as possible.

3. Spread the beetroot slices out on the baking trays and season. Bake the crisps for 1 hour 30 minutes or until crispy, stirring regularly.

4. Transfer the crisps to two large wire racks and leave to cool completely before serving or storing in an airtight container.

133

Coleslaw

SERVES: 6 | PREPARATION TIME: 20 MINUTES

INGREDIENTS

1 red onion, thinly sliced

1 lemon, juiced

2 carrots, peeled

½ small red cabbage, shredded

1 tsp Dijon mustard

100 ml / 3 ½ fl. oz / ½ cup mayonnaise

flat-leaf parsley, to garnish

METHOD

1. Put the onion in a bowl with the lemon juice and a pinch of salt. Stir well and leave to macerate for 15 minutes to soften the flavour and texture.

2. Shred the carrot with a julienne tool, mandolin or coarse grater and toss with the cabbage and onion.

3. Stir the mustard into the mayonnaise, then mix the dressing with the shredded vegetables.

4. Garnish with parsley and serve straight away or store in the fridge.

Scandinavian potato salad

SERVES: 6 | PREP TIME: 15 MINUTES | COOKING TIME: 12 MINUTES

INGREDIENTS

6 medium potatoes, peeled and cut into chunks

4 large eggs

½ lemon, juiced and zest finely grated

150 ml / 5 ½ fl. oz / ⅔ cup mayonnaise

6 radishes, halved and sliced

1 small bunch dill, chopped

METHOD

1. Boil the potatoes in salted water for 12 minutes or until tender to the point of a knife. Drain well and leave to cool.

2. Meanwhile, put the eggs in a small saucepan of cold water. When they start to boil, reduce the heat to its lowest setting and simmer gently for 5 minutes. Plunge the eggs into iced water to cool for 5 minutes, then peel, quarter and slice them.

3. Stir the lemon juice and zest into the mayonnaise and season with salt, then toss with the potatoes, eggs, radishes and dill.

4. Serve immediately at room temperature for the best texture, or store in the fridge until later.

135

Gluten-free granola bars

MAKES: 10 | PREP TIME: 20 MINUTES | COOKING TIME: 25 MINUTES

INGREDIENTS

100 g / 3 ½ oz / ½ cup butter

100 g / 3 ½ oz / ⅓ cup runny honey

75 g / 2 ½ oz / ⅓ cup light muscovado sugar

175 g / 6 oz / 1 ¾ cups rolled buckwheat flakes

50 g / 1 ¾ oz / ½ cup sunflower seeds

50 g / 1 ¾ oz / ½ cup pumpkin seeds

50 g / 1 ¾ oz / ¼ cup sesame seeds

100 g / 3 ½ oz / ¾ cup walnuts, chopped

100 g / 3 ½ oz / ½ cup raisins

50 g / 1 ¾ oz / ½ cup ground almonds

METHOD

1. Preheat the oven to 180°C (160°C fan) / 350F / gas 4 and grease and line a 20 x 30 cm (8 in x 11 in) tray bake tin with greaseproof paper.

2. Put the butter, honey and sugar in a saucepan and melt them together over a low heat until the sugar dissolves. Increase the heat and bubble for 1 minute.

3. Take the pan off the heat and stir in the rest of the ingredients with a pinch of salt.

4. Tip the mixture into the prepared tin and press it into an even layer.

5. Bake in the oven for 25 minutes, or until golden brown.

6. Cut the tray bake into bars while it is still warm, but leave to cool completely in the tin before serving.

Cheese, bacon and spring onion scones

MAKES: 12 | PREP TIME: 15 MINUTES | COOKING TIME: 15 MINUTES

INGREDIENTS

1 tbsp olive oil

3 rashers streaky bacon, finely chopped

75 g / 2 ½ oz / ⅓ cup butter, cubed

150 g / 5 ½ oz / 1 cup self-raising flour,
plus extra for dusting

100 g / 3 ½ oz / ⅔ cup wholemeal flour

½ tsp mustard powder

¼ tsp cayenne pepper

3 spring onions (scallions), chopped

150 ml / 5 ½ fl. oz / ⅔ cup milk,
plus extra for brushing

100 g / 3 ½ oz / 1 cup Red Leicester cheese, grated

METHOD

1. Preheat the oven to 220°C (200°C fan) / 425F / gas 7 and line two baking trays with greaseproof paper.

2. Heat the oil in a frying pan and fry the bacon for 2 minutes or until golden brown. Leave to cool.

3. Rub the butter into the two flours, then stir in the mustard powder, cayenne pepper, spring onions and bacon. Add the milk and ¾ of the cheese and mix together into a soft dough, adding a little more milk if necessary.

4. Divide the dough into 12 equal pieces and shape into rough rounds, then spread them out on the baking trays.

5. Brush the scones with milk, sprinkle with the rest of the cheese and bake for 15 minutes or until golden brown and cooked through.

6. Transfer the scones to a wire rack to cool a little before serving warm.

Pear, walnut and blue cheese salad

SERVES: 2 | PREPARATION TIME: 15 MINUTES

INGREDIENTS

1 ripe conference pear

50 g / 1 ¾ oz / ½ cup walnuts, lightly chopped

75 g / 2 ½ oz gorgonzola cheese, crumbled

50 g / 1 ¾ oz rocket (arugula)

50 g / 1 ¾ oz green leaf lettuce

2 tbsp extra virgin olive oil

1 clove of garlic, minced

1 lemon, juiced

1 tsp Dijon mustard

METHOD

1. Cut the top and bottom from the pear and slice in half to remove the core. Chop the remaining pear into slices.

2. Arrange the pear onto serving plates with the nuts, cheese, rocket and lettuce leaves.

3. Place the oil, garlic, lemon and mustard into a sealable jar. Shake to combine before seasoning with salt and black pepper.

4. Drizzle the dressing over the salad before serving.

140

Sweet potato wedges with onion and feta

SERVES: 4 | PREP TIME: 5 MINUTES | COOKING TIME: 25 MINUTES

INGREDIENTS

3 medium sweet potatoes, peeled and
cut into wedges

1 red onion, peeled and cut into wedges

50 ml / 1 ¾ fl. oz / ¼ cup olive oil

1 lemon, zest finely pared

a few sprigs oregano, stems removed

few sprigs young tender rosemary, stems removed

100 g / 3 ½ oz / ½ cup feta, crumbled

METHOD

1. Preheat the oven to 220°C (200°C fan) / 425F / gas
   7 and line two large baking trays with
   greaseproof paper.

2. Divide the sweet potato wedges and onion
   between the two baking trays, drizzle with oil and
   season with salt and pepper. Toss well to coat.

3. Roast for 25 minutes, turning occasionally, until
   golden brown and cooked through.

4. Transfer the vegetables to a warm serving dish
   and toss with the lemon zest, oregano, rosemary
   and feta. Serve immediately.

141

Homemade chips

SERVES: 4 | PREP TIME: 1 HOUR, 35 MINUTES | COOKING TIME: 15 MINUTE

INGREDIENTS

4 large Maris Piper potatoes, peeled and cut into skinny chips

sunflower oil for deep-frying

ketchup, to serve

METHOD

1. Soak the potatoes in cold water for 1 hour to reduce the starch.

2. Drain the chips and pat dry with a clean tea towel, then air-dry on a wire rack for 30 minutes

3. Heat the oil in a deep fat fryer, according to the manufacturer's instructions, to a temperature o 130°C (265F). Par-cook the chips for 10 minutes so that they cook all the way through but don't brown. Drain the chips on plenty of kitchen paper to absorb the excess oil.

4. Increase the fryer temperature to 190°C (375F).

5. Return the chips to the fryer basket and cook for 4 minutes or until crisp and golden brown.

6. Drain the chips again and serve with ketchup.

Garlic bread

SERVES: 4 | PREP TIME: 10 MINUTES | COOKING TIME: 20 MINUTES

INGREDIENTS

1 baguette

100 g / 3 ½ oz / ½ cup butter, softened

2 cloves of garlic, crushed

2 tbsp parsley, very finely chopped

METHOD

1. Preheat the oven to 200°C (180°C fan) / 400F / gas 6.

2. Slice the baguette on the diagonal without cutting all the way through to the bottom.

3. Mix the butter with the garlic and parsley and season with salt and pepper. Spread the mixture over the cut surfaces of the bread. Wrap the baguette in foil.

4. Bake for 15 minutes, then open up the foil and bake for 5 more minutes.

Winter vegetable and citrus salad

SERVES: 2-4 | PREPARATION TIME: 20 MINUTES

INGREDIENTS

½ red cabbage, shredded

1 tbsp cider vinegar

1 tsp salt

1 lemon, juiced

2 tbsp olive oil

1 orange

1 pink grapefruit

250 g / 9 oz cooked beetroot, sliced

handful of flat leaf parsley, chopped

25 g / 1 oz walnuts, chopped

METHOD

1. Place the cabbage into a bowl with the vinegar, salt, lemon juice and olive oil. Cover and set aside to soften for 8–10 minutes.

2. Peel the orange and grapefruit, divide the segments and remove any seeds.

3. Add the fruit and beetroot to the cabbage and toss to combine the ingredients. Season with salt and black pepper to taste.

4. Stir through the parsley and walnuts before serving.

Kohlrabi fries

SERVES: 2 | PREP TIME: 10 MINUTES | COOKING TIME: 20 MINUTES

INGREDIENTS

2 medium sized kohlrabi (German turnip)

2 tbsp olive oil

1 tsp salt

METHOD

1. Preheat the oven to 220°C (200°C fan) / 425F / gas 7.

2. Remove the leaves from the kohlrabi before topping and tailing. Peel the remaining skin before chopping into wedges and then fries.

3. Toss the fries with the oil and salt and place onto a baking tray.

4. Bake in the hot oven for 20 minutes until crisp.

5. Remove and place onto kitchen paper to absorb any excess oil. Toss with additional salt as desired before serving.

Roasted new potatoes with dil

SERVES: 4 | PREP TIME: 5 MINUTES | COOKING TIME: 55 MINUTES

INGREDIENTS

800 g / 1 lb 12 oz / 6 ½ cups new potatoes, halved (or cut into thirds, if large)

75 ml / 2 ½ fl. oz / ⅓ cup olive oil

2 cloves of garlic, finely chopped

1 small bunch dill, chopped

METHOD

1. Preheat the oven to 200°C (180°C fan) / 400F / gas 6

2. Boil the potatoes in salted water for 10 minutes then drain well and leave to steam dry for 2 minutes. Meanwhile, put the oil in a large roasting tin in the oven to heat.

3. Add the potatoes to the roasting tin and stir to coat in the oil. Season well with salt and pepper.

4. Roast for 20 minutes, then turn them over. Roast for 15 minutes and toss with the garlic, then return to the oven for 10 minutes or until golden brown and crisp.

5. Sprinkle the potatoes with dill just before serving

Dried fruit scones

MAKES: 8 | PREP TIME: 25 MINUTES | COOKING TIME: 20 MINUTES

INGREDIENTS

225 g / 8 oz / 1 ½ cups self-raising flour

55 g / 2 oz / ¼ cup butter

75 g / 2 ½ oz / ½ cup dried mixed fruit

150 ml / 5 fl. oz / ⅔ cup whole milk,
plus extra for brushing

2 tbsp demerara sugar

butter and jam (jelly) to serve

METHOD

1. Preheat the oven to 220°C (200°C fan) / 425F / gas 7 and oil a large baking sheet.

2. Sieve the flour into a bowl and rub in the butter until the mixture resembles fine breadcrumbs. Add the mixed fruit and stir in enough milk to bring the mixture together into a soft dough.

3. Shape the dough into a round loaf approximately 2.5 cm (1 in) thick.

4. Brush the top with milk and sprinkle with sugar. Cut into eight wedges and transfer to the prepared baking sheet.

5. Bake in the oven for 20 minutes or until golden brown on top and cooked through. Transfer the scones to a wire rack to cool a little, then serve warm with butter and jam.

147

Strawberry smoothie

SERVES: 1 | PREPARATION TIME: 5 MINUTES

●●●●●●●●●●●●●●●●●●●●●●●●●●●

INGREDIENTS

100 g / 3 ½ oz / ⅔ cup strawberries, sliced

2 tbsp Greek yogurt

75 ml / 2 ½ fl. oz / ⅓ cup apple juice

1 tsp runny honey

4 ice cubes

METHOD

1. Reserve a few sliced strawberries for a garnish and put the rest in a liquidizer with the rest of the ingredients.

2. Blend for 1 minute or until very smooth.

3. Pour into a glass and garnish with the reserved sliced strawberries.

SIDES AND SNACKS

Green super smoothie

SERVES: 1 | PREP TIME: 5 MINUTES | FREEZING TIME: 2 HOURS

INGREDIENTS

2 bananas, chopped

2 kiwi fruit, peeled and chopped

35 g baby leaf spinach

250 ml / 9 fl. oz / 1 cup apple juice

METHOD

1. Spread the banana and kiwi fruit out on a greaseproof paper lined baking tray and freeze for at least 2 hours. It can then be transferred to a freezer bag and stored for future use or used straight away.

2. Put the spinach in a liquidizer or blender with the apple juice. Blend until smooth.

3. Add the frozen banana and kiwi and blend again until smooth, then pour into a glass and serve immediately.

149

Fig and cashew milkshake

SERVES: 1 | PREPARATION TIME: 5 MINUTES

●●●●●●●●●●●●●●●●●●●●●●●●●●●●

INGREDIENTS

3 fresh figs, chopped, plus extra to garnish

1 handful cashew nuts

250 ml / 9 fl. oz / 1 cup milk

1 tbsp runny honey

2 scoops vanilla ice cream

METHOD

1. Put the figs, cashew nuts, milk and honey in a liquidizer and blend until smooth.

2. Add the ice cream and blend again for 10 seconds.

3. Pour the milkshake into a glass and garnish with a little more fig. Serve immediately.

Pumpkin pancakes

SERVES: 1-2 | PREP TIME: 20 MINUTES | COOKING TIME: 1 HOUR

INGREDIENTS

½ pumpkin

150 g / 5 ¼ oz self-raising flour

1 tsp baking powder

1 tsp ground ginger

1 tsp all spice

50 g / 1 ¾ oz / ¼ cup caster (superfine) sugar

150 ml / 5 ¼ fl. oz / ⅔ cup milk

1 egg

METHOD

1. Preheat the oven to 180°C (160°C fan) / 350F / gas 4.

2. Slice and peel the pumpkin place onto a baking tray. Roast in the oven for 40–45 minutes.

3. Puree the pumpkin in a blender. Leave to cool.

4. In a bowl, stir and combine the dry ingredients.

5. Whisk together the milk and egg until frothy. Combine all of the ingredients in the bowl and mix to form a batter.

6. Heat a little oil in a non-stick frying pan over a medium heat, then add a ladle of the batter to the pan. Cook for 2–3 minutes until bubbles appear on the surface, then flip and cook for a further 2–3 minutes. Transfer to a warm oven.

7. Serve the pancakes with a drizzle of honey, maple syrup or chocolate sauce.

151

Rainbow cookies

MAKES: 24 | PREP TIME: 20 MINUTES | COOKING TIME: 15 MINUTES

INGREDIENTS

225 g / 8 oz / 1 ⅓ cups light brown sugar

100 g / 3 ½ oz / ½ cup caster sugar

175 g / 6 oz / ¾ cup butter, melted

2 tsp vanilla extract

1 egg, plus 1 egg yolk

250 g / 9 oz / 1 ⅔ cups self-raising flour

100 g / 3 ½ oz / ⅔ cup candy-coated chocolate buttons

METHOD

1. Preheat the oven to 160°C (140°C fan) / 325F / gas 3 and line two baking sheets with greaseproof paper.

2. Cream together the two sugars, butter and vanilla extract until pale and well whipped then beat in the egg and yolk, followed by the flour and the candy-coated chocolate buttons.

3. Use an ice cream scoop to portion the mixture onto the prepared trays, leaving plenty of room to spread.

4. Bake the cookies in batches for 15 minutes or until the edges are starting to brown but the centres are still chewy. Transfer to a wire rack and leave to cool.

Gingerbread biscuits

MAKES: 28 | PREP TIME: 1 HOUR, 15 MINUTES | COOKING TIME: 10 MINUTES

INGREDIENTS

100 g / 3 ½ oz / ½ cup soft brown sugar

100 g / 3 ½ oz / ½ cup butter, softened

1 large egg, beaten

300 g / 10 ½ oz / 2 cups plain (all-purpose) flour

2 tsp ground ginger

METHOD

1. Cream together the sugar and butter until pale and well whipped, then beat in the egg followed by the flour and ginger. Bring the mixture together into a ball with your hands, then wrap in cling film and refrigerate for 45 minutes.

2. Preheat the oven to 190°C (170°C fan) / 375F / gas 5 and line two baking tins.

3. Roll out portions of the dough on a lightly floured surface to 3 mm thick. Cut out the biscuits with a fluted cutter, reusing the excess.

4. Transfer the biscuits to the prepared trays in batches and bake for 10 minutes until evenly cooked and golden. Remove to a wire rack and leave to cool completely.

153

Spicy crunch biscuits

MAKES: 24 | PREP TIME: 15 MINUTES | COOKING TIME: 15 MINUTES

INGREDIENTS

75 g / 2 ½ oz / ⅓ cup butter, softened

100 g / 3 ½ oz / ⅓ cup golden syrup

225 g / 8 oz / 1 ½ cups self-raising flour

100 g / 3 ½ oz / ½ cup caster (superfine) sugar

2 tsp ground ginger

1 tsp ground cinnamon

1 large egg, beaten

2 tbsp demerara sugar

METHOD

1. Preheat the oven to 180°C (160°C fan) / 350F / gas 4 and line two baking sheets with greaseproof paper.

2. Melt the butter and golden syrup together in a saucepan. Mix the flour, caster sugar and spices together then stir into the mixture with the beaten egg.

3. Use a teaspoon to portion the mixture onto the baking trays, leaving plenty of room for the biscuits to spread.

4. Sprinkling with demerara sugar and bake for 15 minutes or until golden brown.

5. Transfer the biscuits to a wire rack and leave to cool and harden.

154

Red velvet crinkle cookies

MAKES: 24 | PREP TIME: 20 MINUTES | COOKING TIME: 12 MINUTES

INGREDIENTS

250 g / 9 oz / 1 ¼ cups caster (superfine) sugar

100 g / 3 ½ oz / ½ cup butter, softened

1 tsp vanilla extract

2 tsp red food colouring

2 eggs

250 g / 9 oz / 1 ⅔ cups plain (all-purpose) flour

1 ½ tsp baking powder

30 g unsweetened cocoa powder

100 g / 3 ½ oz / ⅔ cup white chocolate chips

100 g / 3 ½ oz / 1 cup icing (confectioner's) sugar

METHOD

1. Preheat the oven to 180°C (160°C fan) / 350F / gas 4 and line two baking trays with greaseproof paper.

2. Cream together the sugar, butter, vanilla extract and food colouring until pale and well whipped, then beat in the eggs one at a time.

3. Sieve over the flour, baking powder and cocoa and add the chocolate chips, then stir together until evenly mixed.

4. Shape the mixture into 2.5 cm (1 in) balls and roll in icing sugar to coat. Spread out on the prepared trays, leaving plenty of room to spread.

5. Bake the cookies in batches for 12 minutes or until the edges are starting to colour but the centres are still chewy. Transfer to a wire rack and leave to cool before serving.

Oaty wholemeal banana muffins

MAKES: 12 | PREP TIME: 25 MINUTES | COOKING TIME: 18 MINUTES

INGREDIENTS

3 very ripe bananas

110 g / 4 oz / ⅔ cup soft light brown sugar

2 large eggs

120 ml / 4 fl. oz / ½ cup sunflower oil

200 g / 7 oz / 1 ⅓ cups wholemeal flour

2 tsp baking powder

30 g rolled porridge oats, plus extra for sprinkling

METHOD

1. Preheat the oven to 200°C (180°C fan) / 400F / gas 6 and grease a 12-hole silicone cupcake mould

2. Mash the bananas with a fork then whisk in the sugar, eggs and oil.

3. Sieve the flour and baking powder into the bowl and add the oats, stirring enough to evenly mix

4. Add the mix to the mould and sprinkle with oats. Bake for 18 minutes until a skewer inserted comes out clean.

5. Transfer the muffins to a wire rack and leave to cool a little before serving.

Plum and yogurt muffins

MAKES: 12 | PREP TIME: 10 MINUTES | COOKING TIME: 25 MINUTES

INGREDIENTS

200 g / 7 oz / ¾ cup caster (superfine) sugar

00 g / 10 ½ oz / 2 cups self-raising wholemeal flour

250 g / 9 oz natural yogurt

2 large free-range eggs, beaten

1 tsp vanilla extract

100 g / 3 ½ oz plum jam (jelly)

METHOD

1. Preheat the oven to 200°C (180°C fan) / 400F / gas 6 and line a muffin tin with cases.

2. Mix the sugar and flour in a large mixing bowl.

3. In a separate bowl whisk together the yogurt, eggs and vanilla extract.

4. Make a well in the centre of the dry ingredients and pour in the wet. Mix just enough to combine the two.

5. Spoon the mixture into the prepared muffin tin. Bake in the oven for 25 minutes until risen and a skewer inserted into the centre comes out clean. Remove to cool completely.

6. Cut a hole into the top of each muffin and spoon in the plum jam.

159

Wholemeal strawberry muffins

MAKES: 12 | PREP TIME: 10 MINUTES | COOKING TIME: 20 MINUTES

●●●●●●●●●●●●●●●●●●●●●●●●●●●●

INGREDIENTS

200 g / 7 oz / ¾ cup caster (superfine) sugar

300 g / 10 ½ oz / 2 cups self-raising wholemeal flour

250 ml / 9 fl. oz / 1 cup milk

60 g / 2 oz / ¼ cup unsalted butter, melted

2 large free-range eggs, beaten

1 tsp vanilla extract

150 g / 5 ¼ oz strawberries, washed and dehulled

METHOD

1. Preheat the oven to 200°C (180°C fan) / 400F / gas 6 and line a muffin tin with cases.

2. Mix the sugar and flour in a mixing bowl. In another bowl, whisk together everything else, except the strawberries, until frothy.

3. Make a well in the centre of the dry ingredients, pour in the wet and mix just enough to combine.

4. Set 6 strawberries aside. Chop the rest and stir into the muffin mix.

5. Spoon into the cases and bake in the oven for 20 minutes until risen and a skewer comes out clean. Remove to cool completely. Half the remaining strawberries and place on top.

Oat streusel muffins

MAKES: 12 | PREP TIME: 15 MINUTES | COOKING TIME: 30 MINUTES

INGREDIENTS

200 g / 7 oz / ¾ cup golden caster (superfine) sugar

300 g / 10 ½ oz / 2 cups self-raising wholemeal flour

1 tsp cinnamon

250 ml / 9 fl. oz / 1 cup milk

100 g / 3 ½ oz unsalted butter, melted

2 large free-range eggs, beaten

1 tsp vanilla extract

50 g / 1 ¾ oz / ½ cup rolled oats

2 tbsp plain (all purpose) flour

75 g / 2 ½ oz / ½ cup soft brown sugar

METHOD

1. Preheat the oven to 200°C (180°C fan) / 400F / gas 6 and line a muffin tin with cases.

2. Mix the sugar, flour and cinnamon in a large mixing bowl. In a separate bowl, whisk together the milk, half the butter, eggs and vanilla extract until frothy.

3. Make a well in the centre of the dry ingredients, pour in the wet and mix just enough to combine.

4. In a separate bowl combine the oats, flour and brown sugar. Melt the remaining butter in a saucepan and mix to form a sticky topping.

5. Spoon the muffin batter into the prepared tin and top with the oat topping. Bake in the hot oven for 22-25 minutes until golden and a skewer inserted comes out clean.

161

Cook's Corner

Student Cookbook

Desserts

Indulgent mug cakes

MAKES: 2 | PREP TIME: 15 MINUTES | COOKING TIME: 2 MINUTES

INGREDIENTS

55 g / 2 oz / ¼ cup butter, softened

55 g / 2 oz / ¼ cup caster (superfine) sugar

1 large egg

55 g / 2 oz / ⅓ cup self-raising flour, sifted

1 tbsp cocoa powder

50 g / 1 ¾ oz / ⅓ cup dark chocolate (minimum 60% cocoa solids), chopped

2 tbsp double (heavy) cream

1 tbsp dark and white chocolate chips

METHOD

1. Beat the butter and sugar together in a mug until pale and smooth.

2. Break the egg into a second mug and beat gently with a fork, then gradually stir the egg into the butter mixture.

3. Fold in the flour and cocoa powder, followed by 1 tablespoon of the chopped chocolate, then spoon half of the mixture into the mug you used to beat the egg and level the tops.

4. Transfer the mugs to a microwave and cook on full power for 1 minute 30 seconds. Test the cakes by inserting a skewer into the centre – if it comes out clean, they are ready. If not, return to the microwave for 15 seconds and test again.

5. In a separate mug, pour the cream and the rest of the chopped chocolate.

6. Cook on medium power for 20 seconds and stir, then return to the microwave, checking every 10 seconds until the chocolate has melted. Stir until smooth, then drizzle over the cakes and decorate with chocolate chips.

Cherry crumble slices

SERVES: 6-8 | PREP TIME: 20 MINUTES | COOKING TIME: 30 MINUTES

INGREDIENTS

300 g / 10 ½ oz / 2 cups plain (all purpose) flour

250 g / 9 oz / 1 ¼ cups caster (superfine) sugar

1 tsp baking powder

1 tsp salt

250 g / 9 oz / 1 ¼ cups unsalted butter

2 large egg yolks

1 tsp vanilla extract

1 tsp almond extract

100 g / 3 ½ oz / 1 cup ground almonds

400 g / 14 oz pitted black cherries in syrup

METHOD

1. Preheat the oven to 180°C (160°C fan) / 350F / gas 4 and lightly grease and line a baking tray with greaseproof paper.

2. Place the flour, 150 g caster sugar, baking powder and salt into a food processor. Add 150 g of the butter cut into cubes and blend until the mixture resembles breadcrumbs.

3. Whisk together the eggs, vanilla and almond extract. Combine the eggs with the flour mixture and mix until a dough forms, taking care not to overmix.

4. Press the dough into the base of the baking tray so that it covers the whole tray.

5. Add the remaining sugar, butter and ground almonds in a food processor and blend quickly to form a crumble topping.

6. Spread the cherries in their syrup onto the prepared base and sprinkle over the almond topping.

7. Bake in the hot oven for 30 minutes until the topping is golden.

8. Remove to cool before cutting into squares.

Cranachan

SERVES: 4 | PREP TIME: 15 MINUTES | COOKING TIME: 5 MINUTES

INGREDIENTS

85 g / 3 oz / ¾ cup porridge oats

568 ml / 19 ¼ fl. oz / 2 ¼ cups double (heavy) cream

50 ml / 1 ¾ fl. oz / ¼ cup whisky

50 g / 1 ¾ oz / ¼ cup honey

300 g / 10 ½ oz / 2 cups raspberries

mint sprigs to garnish

METHOD

1. Lightly toast the porridge oats in a dry pan taking care not to burn them.

2. Whip the cream until soft peaks form. Fold in the whisky and half the honey.

3. Spoon the cream mixture into serving glasses, top with the oats and the remaining honey.

4. Lightly crush half the raspberries and spoon over the top. Garnish with the remaining whole berries and mint.

Fruit salad

SERVES: 6 | PREPARATION TIME: 5 MINUTES

INGREDIENTS

1 small melon, peeled, deseeded and cut into bite-sized chunks

nectarines, stoned and cut into bite-sized chunks

1 small bunch grapes, stems removed

225 g / 8 oz / 1 ½ cups fresh or frozen berries, defrosted if frozen

mint sprigs, to garnish

METHOD

1. Wash the fruit and dry it using a sheet of kitchen roll.

2. Mix all of the fruits together in a large bowl.

3. Divide between six bowls or wide mugs and garnish with mint.

Summer berry fool

SERVES: 6 | PREP TIME: 15 MINUTES | COOKING TIME: 8 MINUTES

INGREDIENTS

300 g / 10 ½ oz / 2 cups mixed berries, plus a
few extra to garnish

100 g / 3 ½ oz / ½ cup caster (superfine) sugar

300 ml / 10 ½ fl. oz / 1 ¼ cups double (heavy) cream

1 tsp vanilla extract

300 ml / 10 ½ fl. oz / 1 ¼ cups Greek yogurt

mint leaves, to garnish

METHOD

1. Put the berries in a saucepan with the sugar.
   Cover and simmer for 8 minutes, stirring
   half way through.

2. Pass the berries through a sieve to remove
   the seeds and skins and set aside to cool.

3. Whip the cream with the vanilla extract
   until it holds its shape, then fold in the
   cooled berry puree and yogurt.

4. Spoon into six dessert glasses and garnish
   with berries and mint.

Strawberry and kiwi lollies

ERVES: 6 | PREP TIME: 15 MINUTES | FREEZING TIME: 4 HOURS OVERNIGHT

INGREDIENTS

150 g / 5 ¼ oz fresh strawberries

150 g / 5 ¼ oz kiwi fruit

handful of fresh mint leaves, chopped

500 ml / 17 fl. oz / 2 cups coconut water

METHOD

1. Wash the strawberries before dehulling and slicing.

2. Peel the kiwi fruit and slice the flesh.

3. Combine the fruit with the chopped mint and place into lolly moulds.

4. Top up with the coconut water before placing into the freezer for at least 4 hours or overnight until frozen.

171

Fruity chocolate custards

SERVES: 6 | PREP TIME: 10 MINUTES | COOKING TIME: 10 MINUTES

CHILLING TIME: 1 HOUR

INGREDIENTS

450 ml / 12 ½ fl. oz / 1 ¾ cups whole milk

4 large egg yolks

75 g / 2 ½ oz / ⅓ cup caster (superfine) sugar

1 tsp cornflour (cornstarch)

2 tbsp unsweetened cocoa powder

150 g / 5 ½ oz / 1 cup mixed berries

mint sprigs, to garnish

METHOD

1. Put the milk in a saucepan and bring to simmering point.

2. Whisk the egg yolks with the caster sugar, cornflour and cocoa until thick.

3. Gradually incorporate the hot milk, whisking all the time, then scrape the mixture back into the saucepan.

4. Stir the custard over a low heat until it thickens, then divide between six small ramekins.

5. Leave to cool, then chill in the fridge for 1 hour. Serve garnished with berries and mint.

Tiramisu

SERVES: 6 | PREP TIME: 20 MINUTES | CHILLING TIME: 1 HOUR

INGREDIENTS

600 ml / 1 pint / 2 ½ cups double cream

300 g / 10 ½ oz / 1 ⅓ cups mascarpone

4 tbsp icing (confectioner's) sugar

100 ml / 3 ½ fl. oz / ½ cup Marsala wine
or chocolate liqueur

₀0 ml / 3 ½ fl. oz / ½ cup strong filter coffee, cooled

300 g / 10 ½ oz sponge fingers

unsweetened cocoa powder for dusting

METHOD

1. Put the cream, mascarpone and sugar in a bowl with half of the Marsala wine and whip with an electric whisk until it holds its shape.

2. Mix the rest of the Marsala with the coffee. Dip half of the sponge fingers in the coffee mixture and divide between six glass mugs. Spoon half of the cream mixture over the top.

3. Dip the rest of the sponge fingers in the coffee and arrange on top.

4. Spoon over the rest of the cream mixture and dust with cocoa.

5. Chill in the fridge for at least 1 hour before serving.

173

Strawberry verrines

SERVES: 4 | PREP TIME: 20 MINUTES | COOKING TIME: 1 MINUTE
CHILLING TIME: 1 HOUR

INGREDIENTS

135 g / 5 oz / ⅔ cup jelly strawberry (jello) cubes

150 g / 5 ½ oz / 1 cup strawberries, halved

2 tbsp runny honey

1 tsp vanilla extract

500 ml / 17 ½ fl. oz / 2 cups Greek yogurt

METHOD

1. Put the jelly cubes in a microwaveable jug with 100 ml water and microwave on high for 1 minute. Stir to dissolve, then make up to 570 ml with cold water.

2. Stir in the strawberries and set aside.

3. Stir the honey and vanilla into the yogurt and divide a third of the mixture between four glasses.

4. Spoon over a third of the strawberries and half of the jelly liquid, then transfer to the fridge to set for 30 minutes.

5. Spoon another third of the yogurt on top and add a third of the strawberries and the rest of the jelly liquid, then return to the fridge for 30 minutes.

6. Top with the rest of the yogurt and the reserved strawberries and refrigerate until ready to serve.

Black forest cupcakes

MAKES: 12 | PREP TIME: 45 MINUTES | COOKING TIME: 15 MINUTES

INGREDIENTS

110 g / 4 oz / ⅔ cup self-raising flour, sifted

2 tbsp unsweetened cocoa powder

110 g / 4 oz / ½ cup caster (superfine) sugar

110 g / 4 oz / ½ cup butter, softened

2 large eggs

1 tsp almond extract

200 g / 7 oz / ⅔ cup cherry jam (jelly)

TO DECORATE:

300 ml / 10 ½ fl. oz / 1 ¼ cup double (heavy) cream

12 cherries

2 tbsp milk chocolate flakes

METHOD

1. Preheat the oven to 190°C (170°C fan) / 375F / gas 5 and line a 12-hole cupcake tin with paper cases.

2. Combine the flour, cocoa, sugar, butter, eggs and almond extract in a bowl and whisk together for 2 minutes or until smooth.

3. Divide half the mixture between the cases and add a big spoonful of jam to each one.

4. Top with the rest of the cake mixture, then transfer the tin to the oven and bake for 15 minutes or until a skewer inserted comes out clean.

5. Transfer the cakes to a wire rack and leave to cool completely.

6. Whisk the cream until it holds its shape, then spoon or pipe it onto the cakes. Top each one with a cherry and sprinkle with chocolate flakes.

Orange upside down cake

SERVES: 6-8 | PREP TIME: 20 MINUTES | COOKING TIME: 40 MINUTES

INGREDIENTS

2 oranges

100 ml / 3 ½ fl. oz / ½ cup water

300 g / 10 ½ oz / 1 ⅓ cups caster (superfine) sugar

50 g / 1 ¾ oz green glacé cherries, halved

100 g / 3 ½ oz / ½ cup butter

2 eggs, separated

100 g / 3 ½ oz / ⅔ cup self-raising flour

1 tsp baking powder

1 tsp vanilla extract

METHOD

1. Preheat the oven to 180°C (160°C fan) / 350F / gas 4 and lightly grease a 20 cm square cake tin and line with greaseproof paper.

2. Zest the oranges and set aside for later. Cut the remaining peel and pith from the orange and slice into rounds, removing any pips.

3. Heat the water in a saucepan and add 200 g of the sugar. Heat until the sugar dissolves and starts to turn the colour of caramel. Pour into the base of the cake tin and carefully arrange the orange slices inside with some overlapping. Scatter over the glacé cherries.

4. Cream together the remaining sugar with the butter until pale and creamy. Add the egg yolks, one at a time, and mix through. Fold in the orange zest, flour, baking powder and vanilla extract.

5. Whisk the egg whites until stiff peaks form. Fold half the egg white into the batter to loosen before adding the rest, keeping the mixture as airy as possible.

6. Pour the batter into the cake tin and bake in the oven for 35–40 minutes or until a skewer inserted into the centre comes out clean.

7. Remove from the oven and place onto a cooling rack for 15 minutes. Place a plate or chopping board on top of the cake tin and flip over to turn out the cake.

8. Remove the greaseproof paper and serve.

Cherry lattice pie

SERVES: 4-6 | PREP TIME: 30 MINUTES | COOKING TIME: 1 HOUR

INGREDIENTS

500 g / 1 lb 1 oz puff pastry

400 g / 14 oz canned cherries in syrup

100 g / 3 ½ oz / ½ cup soft brown sugar

1 tsp vanilla extract

½ tsp cinnamon

1 tbsp butter

1 egg, beaten

METHOD

1. Preheat the oven to 180°C (160°C fan) / 350F / gas 4.

2. Separate off a quarter of the pastry for the lattice topping. Roll out the remaining pastry and place into an ovenproof pie dish.

3. Place the cherries, sugar, vanilla and cinnamon into a sauce pan and gently heat until the sugar has melted. Stir through the butter to thicken the mixture. Set aside to cool a little.

4. Once cooled place the pie filling into the prepared base.

5. Roll out the remaining pastry to approximately 2mm thickness and to a size that will cover the pie. Carefully cut out a lattice pattern using a sharp knife.

6. Brush the edges of the pie with some of the egg mixture before adding the lattice topping. Carefully press onto the edge of the pie to attached. Brush the lattice with the remaining egg mixture.

7. Bake in the oven for around 45 minutes until crisp and golden.

Salted caramel berry pavlovas

MAKES: 4 | PREP TIME: 30 MINUTES | COOKING TIME: 1 HOUR
COOLING TIME: 1 HOUR

INGREDIENTS

4 large egg whites

110g / 4 oz / 1 cup caster (superfine) sugar

300 ml / 10 ½ fl. oz / 1 ¼ cups double (heavy) cream

300 g / 10 ½ oz / 2 cups mixed summer berries

mint sprigs, to garnish

FOR THE SALTED CARAMEL SAUCE:

100 g / 3 ½ oz / ½ cup butter

100 g / 3 ½ oz / ½ cup muscovado sugar

100 g / 3 ½ oz / ⅓ cup golden syrup

100 ml / 3 ½ fl. oz / ½ cup double cream

½ tsp sea salt

METHOD

1. Preheat the oven to 140°C (120°C fan) / 275F / gas 1 and oil and line two large baking trays with greaseproof paper.

2. Whisk the egg whites until stiff, then gradually whisk in half of the sugar until the mixture is very shiny. Fold in the remaining sugar then spread the mixture into six discs on each baking tray.

3. Transfer the trays to the oven and bake for 1 hour, then turn off the heat and leave them to cool completely in the oven.

4. While the meringues are cooling, put all of the sauce ingredients in a small saucepan and stir over a low heat until the sugar dissolves.

5. Bring to the boil then take off the heat and leave to cool.

6. When you're ready to serve, whip the cream until it just holds its shape and sandwich the meringues together in threes, decorating with berries as you go.

7. Drizzle a little sauce over each one and garnish with mint, then serve the rest of the sauce on the side.

Apricot cheesecake

SERVES: 8 | PREP TIME: 30 MINUTES | COOKING TIME: 50 MINUTES
SETTING TIME: 4 HOURS

INGREDIENTS

250 g / 9 oz digestive biscuits

150 g / 5 ¼ oz / ⅔ cup unsalted butter, melted

300 g / 10 ½ oz / 1 ⅓ cups caster (superfine) sugar

500 g / 1 lb 1 oz cream cheese

150 ml / 5 ¼ fl. oz / ⅔ cup double (heavy) cream

1 tsp vanilla extract

4 eggs

2 x gelatine leaf sheets

2 x 400 g / 14 oz canned apricots in syrup

mint, to garnish

METHOD

1. Preheat the oven to 160°C (140°C fan) / 325F / gas 3.

2. Place the biscuits into a bag and crush them using a rolling pin. Mix them with the melted butter and 50 g sugar and press the mixture into a 20 cm spring-form cake tin.

3. Mix the remaining sugar with the cream cheese, cream, vanilla and eggs. Whisk to combine.

4. Pour the filling into the prepared cake tin and bake in the oven for around 50 minutes until the filling is set. Remove and allow to cool.

5. Place the gelatine sheets into cold water to soften.

6. Pour the syrup from the apricots into a saucepan and gently heat. Squeeze the excess moisture from the gelatine sheet and stir into the syrup until they melt, remove from the heat to cool.

7. Pour the syrup on top of the cheesecake whilst it is still in its tin and place the apricot halves on top. Place into the refrigerator to set for at least 4 hours. Garnish with the mint leaves before serving.

Churros and hot chocolate

SERVES: 6 | PREP TIME: 20 MINUTES | COOKING TIME: 30 MINUTES

INGREDIENTS

100 g / 3 ½ oz / ½ cup butter

150 g / 5 ½ oz / 1 cup plain (all-purpose) flour

3 medium eggs, beaten

75 g / 2 ½ oz / ⅓ cup caster (superfine) sugar

sunflower oil, for deep-frying

FOR THE HOT CHOCOLATE:

500 ml / 17 ½ fl. oz / 2 cups whole milk

100 g / 3 ½ oz / ⅔ cup dark chocolate
(min. 60 per cent cocoa solids), grated

1 tbsp cornflour (cornstarch)

50 g / 1 ¾ oz / ¼ cup caster (superfine) sugar

METHOD

1. Heat the butter in a saucepan with 250 ml of water and a pinch of salt. When it boils rapidly, beat in the flour, then stir over a low heat until it forms a ball that leaves the pan clean.

2. Take the saucepan off the heat and leave to cool a little, then beat in the eggs.

3. Heat the oil in a deep fat fryer, according to the manufacturer's instructions, to a temperature of 180°C (350F).

4. Transfer the churros mixture to a piping bag fitted with a large star nozzle. Pipe four 10 cm (4 in) strips of dough into the hot oil and cook for 4 minutes, turning halfway through.

5. Remove the churros from the fryer and drain on kitchen paper, then roll in caster sugar to coat. Continue to fry the churros in batches of four until all the mixture has been used.

6. Meanwhile, heat 400 ml of milk until it starts to simmer, then whisk in the grated chocolate. Stir the cornflour into the remaining 100 ml of cold milk, then stir it into the pan with the sugar. Continue to stir until the chocolate thickens, then divide between six cups and serve with the churros.

Individual apple crumbles

MAKES: 6 | PREP TIME: 20 MINUTES | COOKING TIME: 30 MINUTES

INGREDIENTS

2 large Bramley apples, peeled, cored and chopped

2 tbsp caster (superfine) sugar

75 g / 2 ½ oz / ⅓ cup butter

100 g / 3 ½ oz / ⅔ cup plain (all purpose) flour

25 g ground almonds

40 g light brown sugar

METHOD

1. Preheat the oven to 180°C (160°C fan) / 350F / gas 4.

2. Mix the apples with the caster sugar and divide between six individual baking dishes or large ramekins.

3. Rub the butter into the flour and stir in the ground almonds and brown sugar. Squeeze a handful of the mixture into a clump and then crumble it over the fruit. Use up the rest of the topping in the same way, then shake the dishes to level the tops.

4. Bake the crumbles for 30 minutes or until the topping is golden brown and the fruit is bubbling.

188

Strawberry and amaretti creams

SERVES: 6 | PREPARATION TIME: 15 MINUTES

INGREDIENTS

300 ml / 10 ½ fl. oz / 1 ¼ cups double (heavy) cream

2 tbsp icing (confectioner's) sugar

1 tsp vanilla extract

300 ml / 10 ½ fl. oz / 1 ¼ cups Greek yogurt

100 g / 3 ½ oz / 2 cups amaretti biscuits, crushed

150 g / 5 ½ oz / 1 cup strawberries, cut into quarters

50 ml / 1 ¾ fl. oz / ¼ cup amaretto liqueur

METHOD

1. Whip the cream with the icing sugar and vanilla extract until it holds its shape, then fold in the yogurt.

2. Divide half of the mixture between six glasses and top with half of the biscuits and strawberries. Drizzle with half of the liqueur.

3. Repeat to make a second layer of the ingredients and serve immediately.

189

Summer berry chia seed dessert

SERVES: 2-4 | PREPARATION TIME: 4 HOURS OR OVERNIGHT

INGREDIENTS

½ cup chia seeds

700ml / 24 fl. oz / 2 cups of coconut milk

3 tsp of coconut nectar

1 tsp vanilla extract

50 g / 1 ¾ oz / ⅓ cup strawberries, sliced

50 g / 1 ¾ oz / ⅓ cup blueberries

METHOD

1. Combine the chia seeds, coconut milk, coconut nectar and vanilla extract in a bowl.

2. Cover and refrigerate for at least 4 hours or overnight until the seeds have absorbed the liquid and expanded.

3. Spoon the chia seeds into serving glasses lined with the sliced strawberries and with blueberries in the base.

4. Top with further blueberries and serve.

Blueberry smoothie lollies

SERVES: 4 | PREP TIME: 10 MINUTES | FREEZING TIME: 3 HOURS

INGREDIENTS

225 g / 8 oz / 1 ½ cups blueberries

400 ml / 14 fl. oz / 1 ⅔ cups Greek yogurt

2 tbsp runny honey

METHOD

1. Put all of the ingredients in a liquidizer and blend until smooth.

2. Divide between four disposable plastic cups and transfer to the freezer for 1 hour.

3. Insert a lolly stick into the centre of each one and freeze for a further 2 hours or until solid.

4. Dip the outside of each cup briefly in hot water to unmould before serving.

Individual cherry cheesecake

MAKES: 4 | PREP TIME: 20 MINUTES | SETTING TIME: 4 HOURS

● ●

INGREDIENTS

250 g / 9 oz digestive biscuits

100 g / 3 ½ oz butter, melted

400 g / 14 oz full fat cream cheese

1 lemon, juiced

150 g / 5 ¼ oz / ⅔ cup caster (superfine) sugar

½ tsp vanilla extract

250 ml / 9 fl. oz / 1 cup double (heavy) cream

200 g / 7 oz fresh cherries, pitted

METHOD

1. Place the biscuits into a bag and crush them with a rolling pin. Move to a bowl mix in the melted butter to form a buttery base. Spoon into individual serving bowls and press down firmly.

2. Beat together the cheese, lemon, sugar and vanilla extract until thickened. Whisk in the cream until soft peaks form.

3. Gently heat ¾ of the cherries in a saucepan until they release their juices. Allow to cool before folding through the cream cheese mixture.

4. Spoon the mixture on top of the bases and place into the refrigerator for at least 4 hours to set.

5. Serve with the remaining cherries as a garnish.

Cookie mug cakes

MAKES: 2 | PREP TIME: 10 MINUTES | COOKING TIME: 1 HOUR 30 MINUTES

INGREDIENTS

55 g / 2 oz / ¼ cup butter, softened

55 g / 2 oz / ¼ cup caster (superfine) sugar

1 large egg

5 chocolate sandwich cookies

55 g / 2 oz / ⅓ cup self-raising flour, sifted

METHOD

1. Beat the butter and sugar together in a large mug until pale and smooth. Break the egg into a second mug and beat gently with a fork, then gradually stir the egg into the butter mixture.

2. Crumble four of the cookies and fold them in with the flour. Spoon half of the mixture into the mug you used to beat the egg and level the tops.

3. Transfer the mugs to a microwave and cook on full power for 1 minute 30 seconds. If a skewer comes out clean, they are ready. If not, return to the microwave for 15 seconds and test again.

4. Leave the cakes to cool for 5 minutes, then break the final cookie into pieces on top and serve.

Chocolate mousse crêpes

SERVES: 4 | PREP TIME: 45 MINUTES | COOKING TIME: 20 MINUTES

INGREDIENTS

100 ml / 3 ½ fl. oz / ½ cup double (heavy) cream

100 g / 3 ½ oz / ⅔ cup milk chocolate, chopped

1 large egg white

2 tbsp caster (superfine) sugar

whipped cream, to serve

FOR THE CRÊPES:

150 g / 5 ½ oz / 1 cup plain (all purpose) flour

1 large egg

325 ml / 11 ½ fl. oz / 1 ⅓ cups whole milk

1 tbsp butter

METHOD

1. Heat the cream to simmering point then pour it over the chocolate and stir until smooth. Leave to cool for 10 minutes.

2. Whip the egg whites until stiff then whisk in the sugar. Stir a big spoonful of egg white into the cooled chocolate mixture then fold in the rest with a big metal spoon, keeping as many of the air bubbles intact as possible. Chill in the fridge while you make the pancakes.

3. Sieve the flour into a bowl and make a well in the centre. Break in the egg and pour in the milk then use a whisk to gradually incorporate all of the flour from around the outside.

4. Melt the butter in a small frying pan then whisk it into the batter. Put the buttered frying pan back over a low heat. Add a small ladle of batter and swirl the pan to coat the bottom.

5. When it starts to dry and curl up at the edges, turn the crêpe over with a spatula and cook the other side until golden brown.

6. Repeat with the rest of the mixture then fill the crêpes with three quarters of the chocolate mousse. Put the rest in a piping bag and pipe it over the top.

7. Serve with whipped cream.

Iced lemon drizzle cake

SERVES: 8 | PREP TIME: 20 MINUTES | COOKING TIME: 45 MINUTES

INGREDIENTS

150 g / 5 ½ oz / 1 cup self-raising flour

150 g / 5 ½ oz / ⅔ cup caster (superfine) sugar

150 g / 5 ½ oz / ⅔ cup butter, softened

3 large eggs

1 tsp baking powder

2 lemons, juiced and zest finely grated

100 g / 3 ½ oz / ½ cup granulated sugar

FOR THE ICING:

100 g / 3 ½ oz / ½ cup icing (confectioner's) sugar

1-2 tbsp lemon juice

4 slices crystallized lemon (optional)

METHOD

1. Preheat the oven to 180°C (160°C fan) / 350F / gas 4 and grease and line a loaf tin with greaseproof paper.

2. Put the flour, caster sugar, butter, eggs, baking powder and lemon zest in a large mixing bowl and whisk with an electric whisk for 4 minutes or until pale and well whipped.

3. Scrape the mixture into the tin and level the top with a spatula.

4. Bake for 45 minutes or until a skewer inserted into the centre comes out clean.

5. While the cake is baking, stir the juice of the two lemons into the granulated sugar. As soon as the cake is ready, prick it with a skewer and spoon the syrup over the top.

6. Leave to cool completely.

7. Sieve the icing sugar into a bowl and add just enough lemon juice to make a thick glacé icing. Spoon the icing over the cake and decorate with crystallised lemon slices.

Pecan and marshmallow brownies

MAKES: 9 | PREP TIME: 20 MINUTES | COOKING TIME: 35 MINUTES

INGREDIENTS

100 g / 3 ½ oz / ⅔ cup dark chocolate (minimum 70% cocoa solids), chopped

g / 3 oz / ¾ cup unsweetened cocoa powder, sifted

225 g / 8 oz / 1 cup butter

450 g / 1 lb / 2 ½ cups light brown sugar

4 large eggs

100 g / 3 ½ oz / 1 cup self-raising flour

75 g / 2 ½ oz / ½ cup milk chocolate chips

5 g / 2 ½ oz / ½ cup pecan nuts, roughly chopped

75 g / 2 ½ oz / 1 ¼ cups mini marshmallows

METHOD

1. Preheat the oven to 160°C (140°C fan) / 325F / gas 3 and oil and line a 20 cm (8 in) square cake tin with greaseproof paper.

2. Melt the chocolate, cocoa and butter together in a saucepan, then leave to cool a little.

3. Whisk the sugar and eggs together with an electric whisk for 3 minutes or until very light and creamy. Pour in the chocolate mixture and sieve over the flour, then add the chocolate chips and half of the pecans. Fold together until evenly mixed, being careful not to knock out too much air.

4. Scrape into the prepared tin and sprinkle over the marshmallows and reserved nuts.

5. Bake for 35 minutes or until the outside is set, but the centre is still quite soft, as it will continue to cook in the residual heat.

6. Leave the brownie to cool completely before cutting into nine squares.

199

Banana smoothie ice cream

MAKES: 800 ML | PREP TIME: 15 MINUTES | FREEZING TIME: 3 HOURS

INGREDIENTS

4 ripe bananas, sliced, plus extra to garnish

500 ml / 17 ½ fl. oz / 2 cups natural yogurt

250 ml / 9 fl. oz / 1 cup milk

2 tbsp runny honey

2 tbsp pecan nuts, chopped

2 tbsp milk chocolate, grated

mint leaves, to garnish

METHOD

1. Put the bananas in a liquidizer or blender with the yogurt, milk and honey, then blend until very smooth.

2. Pour the smoothie into a plastic box with a lid and freeze for 2 hours.

3. Scrape the semi-frozen mixture into a food processor and blend until smooth, then return it to the plastic box and freeze for 1 hour.

4. Whizz the mixture in the food processor again, then freeze until completely firm.

5. Scoop the ice cream into bowls and garnish with sliced banana, chopped pecans, grated chocolate and mint sprigs.

Spiced coffee and walnut muffins

MAKES: 12 | PREP TIME: 45 MINUTES | COOKING TIME: 20 MINUTES

INGREDIENTS

1 large egg

120 ml / 4 fl. oz / ½ cup sunflower oil

120 ml / 4 fl. oz / ½ cup strong coffee, cooled

375 g / 12 ½ oz / 2 ½ cups self-raising flour, sifted

1 tsp baking powder

200 g / 7 oz / ¾ cup dark brown sugar

1 tsp ground cinnamon

½ tsp ground star anise

75 g / 2 ½ oz / ⅔ cup walnuts, chopped

300 ml / 10 ½ fl. oz / 1 ¼ cups double (heavy) cream

2 tbsp caramel sauce

METHOD

1. Preheat the oven to 180°C (160°C fan) / 350F / gas 4 and line a 12-hole muffin tin with paper cases.

2. Beat the egg in a jug with the oil and coffee until well mixed.

3. Mix the flour, baking powder, sugar, spices and all but 2 tablespoons of the walnuts in a bowl. Pour in the egg mixture and stir just enough to combine.

4. Spoon the mixture into the cases, then bake in the oven for 20 minutes or until a skewer inserted comes out clean. Transfer the cakes to a wire rack and leave to cool completely.

5. Whip the cream until it holds its shape, then spoon it into a piping bag fitted with a large star nozzle. Pipe a big swirl on top of each cake.

6. Drizzle the muffins with caramel sauce and garnish with the reserved walnuts.

Banana loaf cake

SERVES: 8 | PREP TIME: 15 MINUTES | COOKING TIME: 50 MINUTES

INGREDIENTS

4 very ripe bananas

100 g / 3 ½ oz / ½ cup soft light brown sugar

2 large eggs

125 ml / 4 ½ fl. oz / ½ cup sunflower oil

225 g / 8 oz / 1 ½ cups plain (all purpose) flour

3 tsp baking powder

METHOD

1. Preheat the oven to 160°C (140°C fan) / 325F / gas 3 and line a loaf tin with greaseproof paper.

2. Mash three of the bananas roughly with a fork then whisk in the sugar, eggs and oil.

3. Sieve the flour and baking powder into the bowl and stir just enough to evenly mix all of the ingredients together.

4. Scrape the mixture into the loaf tin.

5. Cut the final banana in half lengthways and press it into the top. Bake for 50 minutes or until a skewer inserted comes out clean.

6. Transfer the cake to a wire rack and leave to cool completely.

Strawberry sponge cake

SERVES: 8 | PREP TIME: 20 MINUTES | COOKING TIME: 35 MINUTES

INGREDIENTS

100 g / 3 ½ oz / ⅓ cups self-raising flour

100 g / 3 ½ oz / ½ cup caster (superfine) sugar

100 g / 3 ½ oz / ½ cup butter, softened

2 large eggs

1 tsp baking powder

1 tsp vanilla extract

100 g / 3 ½ oz / ⅔ cup strawberries, halved or quartered if large

icing (confectioner's) sugar for dusting

METHOD

1. Preheat the oven to 180°C (160° fan) / 350F / gas 4 and grease a 20 cm (8in) round cake tin or ovenproof frying pan.

2. Put the flour, sugar, butter, eggs, baking powder and vanilla extract in a bowl and whisk with an electric whisk for 4 minutes or until pale and well whipped.

3. Fold in the strawberries, then scrape into the prepared tin and level the top with a spatula.

4. Bake for 35 minutes or until a skewer inserted comes out clean.

5. Transfer the cake to a wire rack and leave to cool completely.

6. Dust with icing sugar just before serving.

7. Delicious served with whipped cream.

Strawberry parfait

SERVES: 4 | PREPARATION TIME: 15 MINUTES

INGREDIENTS

500 g / 1 lb 1 oz natural yogurt

1 tbsp honey

1 tsp vanilla extract

250 ml / 9 fl. oz / 1 cup whipped cream

1 banana sliced

100 g / 3 ½ oz strawberries, sliced

50 g / 1 ¾ oz / ½ cup walnuts, chopped

METHOD

1. Whip together the yogurt with the honey and vanilla extract. Taste to check sweetness and adjust accordingly.

2. Spoon the yogurt into serving glasses and place into the refrigerator until needed.

3. Before serving top the yogurt with whipped cream, sliced banana, strawberries and nuts.

Summer fruit rice pudding

SERVES: 6 | PREP TIME: 40 MINUTES | COOKING TIME: 1 HOUR, 30 MINUTES

INGREDIENTS

110 g / 4 oz / ½ cup short grain rice

75 g / 2 ½ oz / ⅓ cup caster (superfine) sugar

1.2 litres / 2 pints / 4 ½ cups whole milk

1 tsp ground cinnamon

150 g / 5 ½ oz / 1 cup blueberries

1 nectarine, stoned and sliced

6 mint sprigs

METHOD

1. Preheat the oven to 140°C (120°C fan) / 275F / gas 1.

2. Stir the rice and sugar into the milk in a baking dish, then cover and bake for 1 hour 30 minutes. Leave to stand for 30 minutes.

3. Divide the rice pudding between six bowls and sprinkle with cinnamon.

4. Top with blueberries, nectarine and mint. Serve warm or chilled.

Blueberry jam cupcakes

MAKES: 12 | PREP TIME: 20 MINUTES | COOKING TIME: 15 MINUTES

INGREDIENTS

110 g / 4 oz / ⅔ cup self-raising flour, sifted

110 g / 4 oz / ½ cup caster (superfine) sugar

110 g / 4 oz / ½ cup butter, softened

2 large eggs

1 tsp vanilla extract

100 ml / 3 ½ fl. oz / ½ cup blueberry jam (jelly)

fresh blueberries, to serve

METHOD

1. Preheat the oven to 190°C (170°C fan) / 375F / gas 5 and line a 12-hole cupcake tin with paper cases.

2. Combine the flour, sugar, butter, eggs and vanilla extract in a bowl and whisk together for 2 minutes or until smooth.

3. Divide the mixture between the cases and add a spoonful of jam to each one.

4. Bake for 15 minutes or until a skewer inserted into the sponge comes out clean.

5. Transfer the cakes to a wire rack and leave to cool completely, before serving with fresh blueberries.

Vanilla cheesecake with berries

SERVES: 8 | PREP TIME: 20 MINUTES | COOKING TIME: 50 MINUTES

INGREDIENTS

200 g / 7 oz / 1 ⅓ cups shortbread, crushed

50 g / 1 ¾ oz / ¼ cup butter, melted

600 g / 1 lb 5 oz / 2 ¾ cups cream cheese

150 ml / 5 fl. oz / ⅔ cup soured cream

175 g / 6 oz / ¾ cup caster (superfine) sugar

2 large eggs, plus 1 egg yolk

2 tbsp plain (all purpose) flour

1 tsp vanilla extract

150 g / 5 ½ oz / 1 cup mixed berries

mint sprigs, to garnish

METHOD

1. Preheat the oven to 180°C (160°C fan) / 350F / gas 4.

2. Grease a 23 cm (9 in) round loose-bottomed tart case. Mix the biscuit crumbs with the butter and press into an even layer across the bottom and sides of the tin.

3. Whisk together the remaining ingredients, except for the berries and mint, until smooth.

4. Spoon the cheesecake mixture on top of the biscuit base and bake for 50 minutes or until the centre is only just set. Leave to cool completely in the tin.

5. Transfer the tin to the fridge and chill for 2 hours, then unmould and decorate with berries and mint.

211

Peppermint cream cupcakes

MAKES: 12 | PREP TIME: 45 MINUTES | COOKING TIME: 15 MINUTES

INGREDIENTS

110 g / 4 oz / ⅔ cup self-raising flour, sifted

110 g / 4 oz / ½ cup caster (superfine) sugar

110 g / 4 oz / ½ cup butter, softened

2 large eggs

½ tsp peppermint extract

100 g / 3 ½ oz / ⅔ cup white chocolate chips

TO DECORATE:

)0 ml / 10 ½ fl. oz / 1 ¼ cup double (heavy) cream

50 g / 1 ¾ oz / ½ cup icing (confectioner's) sugar

½ tsp peppermint extract

mint sprigs, to garnish

METHOD

1. Preheat the oven to 190°C (170°C fan) / 375F / gas 5 and line a 12-hole cupcake tin with paper cases.

2. Combine the flour, sugar, butter, eggs and peppermint extract in a bowl and whisk together for 2 minutes or until smooth. Fold in the chocolate chips then divide the mixture between the paper cases.

3. Bake for 15 minutes or until a skewer inserted comes out clean.

4. Transfer the cakes to a wire rack and leave to cool completely.

5. Whisk the cream with the icing sugar and peppermint extract until it holds its shape, then spoon into a piping bag fitted with a large star nozzle.

6. Pipe a big swirl onto each cake, then garnish with mint sprigs.

Chocolate muffins

MAKES: 12 | PREP TIME: 25 MINUTES | COOKING TIME: 20 MINUTES

INGREDIENTS

1 large egg

120 ml / 4 fl. oz / ½ cup sunflower oil

120 ml / 4 fl. oz / ½ cup milk

375 g / 12 ½ oz / 2 ½ cups self-raising flour, sifted

1 tsp baking powder

200 g / 7 oz / ¾ cup caster (superfine) sugar

100 g / 3 ½ oz / ⅔ cup dark chocolate, min. 60 per cent cocoa solids, chopped

METHOD

1. Preheat the oven to 180°C (160°C fan) / 350F / gas 4 and line a 12-hole muffin tin with paper cases.

2. Beat the egg in a jug with the oil and milk until well mixed.

3. Mix the flour, baking powder and sugar in a bowl, then pour in the egg mixture and chopped chocolate and stir just enough to combine.

4. Divide the mixture between the paper cases, then bake in the oven for 20 minutes. If a skewer inserted comes out clean, the cakes are done. If not, return to the oven for 5 minutes and test again.

5. Transfer the cakes to a wire rack and leave to cool before serving.

Gluten-free black bean brownies

MAKES: 9 | PREP TIME: 15 MINUTES | COOKING TIME: 20 MINUTES

INGREDIENTS

50 g / 1 ¾ oz / ½ cup rolled porridge oats

2 tbsp unsweetened cocoa or cacao powder

1 tsp baking powder

400 g / 14 oz / 2 cups canned black beans, drained and rinsed

100 g / 3 ½ oz / ½ cup soft brown sugar

50 g / 1 ¾ oz / ¼ cup butter, melted

100 g / 3 ½ oz / ⅔ cup dark chocolate (min. 60 per cent cocoa solids), finely chopped

METHOD

1. Preheat the oven to 180°C (160°C fan) / 350F / gas 4.

2. Oil and line a 20 cm (8 in) square cake tin with greaseproof paper.

3. Put the oats, cocoa and baking powder in a food processor and blitz to a combined powder. Add the black beans, sugar, butter and chocolate, then blend again until very smooth.

4. Scrape the mixture into the tin and level the top.

5. Bake for 20 minutes or until the outside is set, but the centre is still quite soft.

6. Leave the brownie to cool completely before cutting and serving.

Apple and cinnamon rolls

MAKES: 9 | PREP TIME: 2 HOURS, 30 MINUTES | COOKING TIME: 35 MINUTES

INGREDIENTS

400 g / 14 oz / 2 ⅔ cups strong white bread flour

½ tsp easy blend dried yeast

4 tbsp caster (superfine) sugar

1 tsp fine sea salt

1 tbsp olive oil

75 g / 2 ½ oz / ½ cup light brown sugar

1 ½ tsp ground cinnamon

25 g butter, softened

1 eating apple, peeled, cored and chopped

1 egg, beaten

METHOD

1. Combine the flour, yeast, caster sugar and salt. Stir the oil into 280 ml of warm water then stir it into the dry ingredients. Knead the dough on an oiled surface for 10 minutes or until smooth and elastic.

2. Leave the dough to rest in a lightly oiled bowl, covered with oiled cling film, for 1-2 hours or until doubled in size. Knead the dough for 2 more minutes, then roll out into a large rectangle.

3. Cream the brown sugar, cinnamon and butter together. Spread the mixture over the dough, then scatter over the apple and roll it up tightly. Cut the roll into nine even slices and arrange them in a round cake tin or ovenproof frying pan.

4. Cover the rolls with oiled cling film and leave to prove for 1 hour or until doubled in size.

5. Preheat the oven to 220°C (200°C fan) / 425F / gas 7.

6. Brush the rolls with egg then transfer the tray to the top shelf of the oven and bake for 35 minutes or until cooked through.

Choc-chip blondies

MAKES: 10 | PREP TIME: 25 MINUTES | COOKING TIME: 35 MINUTES

INGREDIENTS

100 g / 3 ½ oz / ⅔ cup white chocolate, chopped

225 g / 8 oz / 1 cup butter

450 g / 15 ½ oz light brown sugar

4 large eggs

100 g / 3 ½ oz / ⅔ cup self-raising flour

100 g / 3 ½ oz / ⅔ cup milk chocolate chips

75 g / 2 ½ oz / ⅔ cup almonds, chopped

METHOD

1. Preheat the oven to 180°C (160°C fan) / 350F / gas 4 and oil and line a 20 cm x 20 cm square cake tin.

2. Melt the white chocolate and butter together in a saucepan, then leave to cool a little.

3. Whisk together the sugar and eggs with an electric whisk for 3 minutes or until very light and creamy.

4. Pour in the chocolate mixture and sieve over the flour, then fold everything together with the chocolate chips and almonds until evenly mixed.

5. Scrape into the tin and bake for 35 minutes or until the outside is set, but the centre is still quite soft, as it will continue to cook as it cools.

6. Leave the blondie to cool completely before cutting into 10 pieces.

INDEX